OEDIPUS

SUNY SERIES IN CONTEMPORARY FRENCH THOUGHT

David Pettigrew and François Raffoul, editors

OEDIPUS

The Most Crucial Concept in Psychoanalysis

JUAN-DAVID NASIO

Translated by
David Pettigrew and François Raffoul

Originally published as *L'Oedipe : Le concept le plus crucial de la psychanalyse*

© 2005, Editions Payot & Rivages

Published by State University of New York Press, Albany

© 2010 State University of New York

For information, contact State University of New York Press, Albany, NY
www.sunypress.edu

Production by Ryan Morris
Marketing by Anne M. Valentine

Library of Congress Cataloging-in-Publication Data

Nasio, Juan-David.
  [Œdipe. English]
  Oedipus : the most crucial concept in psychoanalysis / Juan-David Nasio ; translated by David Pettigrew and François Raffoul.
    p. cm. -- (SUNY series in contemporary French thought)
  Includes bibliographical references and index.
  ISBN 978-1-4384-3360-8 (paperback : alk. paper)
  ISBN 978-1-4384-3361-5 (hardcover : alk. paper) 1. Oedipus complex. 2. Psychoanalysis. I. Title.
  BF175.5.O33N3713 2010
  150.19'5--dc22
                                2010004842
                  10 9 8 7 6 5 4 3 2 1

Contents

Translators' Acknowledgments

We would first like to thank Jane Bunker, editor in chief at SUNY Press, for her steadfast support throughout.

At Louisiana State University (LSU), we would like to thank Andrea Conque-Johnson, Megan Lann, and Jason Rose for their careful assistance with the review of the manuscript. In addition, our thanks to the staff in the philosophy department at LSU, Jen O'Connor and Margaret Toups, for all their help.

The translation work benefited from Connecticut State University research grants. At Southern Connecticut State University (SCSU), we are grateful to Dr. DonnaJean Fredeen, Dean of the School of Arts and Sciences, for an award of research reassigned time. Thanks as well to the SCSU Office of Sponsored Programs and Research. SCSU Philosophy Department Chairperson, Armen Marsoobian, and Department Secretary, Ms. Sheila Magnotti, offered support and assistance at every stage of the process.

We are especially grateful to Pierre Jacerme, Françoise Delbarry, and Cathy Leblanc, for their help with the translation of key terms. Our gratitude also goes to Melida Badilla for her support during the translation work.

Finally, we are especially grateful to Dr. Nasio for his support and advice throughout the project.

Preface to the American Edition

An Interview with Dr. Nasio
conducted by David Pettigrew and François Raffoul

You were one of the first psychoanalysts to be awarded the prestigious distinction of Chevalier de la Légion d'Honneur. How has this honor affected your work?
It has already been ten years since I received this title, and since then, I feel, more than ever, that I am among those who by their work and by their passion build the France of today. I was born in Argentina, but if Argentina was my "roots," France is, for me, my "fertile soil." It is above all our beautiful French language, this clay that I shape with joy and pain each time that I write, this living material whose breath punctuates my thinking, molds my writing, and fine-tunes my listening as a psychoanalyst.

For a psychoanalyst, who needs to use a language as a tool, has it been a problem to work in another language? How did it happen that you have mastered French so perfectly?
That is a secret! When I arrived in Paris, I did not know one word of French! In the beginning, I did what everyone else does and I went to study French at the *Alliance Française*. Later, the first book I read was Lacan's *Écrits*, a text that is complicated and difficult to read, even for a French person. If you opened my old copy of *Écrits* you would see that most of the words are translated and written in pencil in Spanish in the margins. Also, I imitated Demosthenes, who had a speech impediment, and was said to have placed stones in his mouth in order to learn to speak. This is how he became one of the most celebrated orators of

ancient Greece. For my part, I put these hard "Lacanian" stones in my mouth in order to learn to speak French! But it was not reading such a difficult work that most helped me to assimilate French. No. Here is the real secret: I would sit for hours and hours copying the greatest texts of French literature. I copied constantly, all the time, like the medieval monks who spent their lives copying the Bible. I told myself, "You must get it, the French must enter, enter the body, through all the pores of the skin!" It was thus that I copied and copied, at times blindly, at times without understanding the text. I recopied the most beautiful pages of Maupassant, Victor Hugo, Mallarmé, and many other great authors of our literature. It was necessary for the French to enter into me, not only through my eyes, but also through my hand. Thus charged with literary energy, I was like the little toy cars that one winds up and that flies into motion as soon as one releases them. My adopted language thus became spontaneous. In 1969, when I arrived in France, I wrote my papers in Spanish, but after 1970, I never wrote another line in my mother tongue. Since then I only write in French.

Do you dream in French?
Yes, indeed. I feel impregnated by this language that possesses so many nuances, a rich vocabulary, and an eminently logical syntax conducive to the clear expression of an idea. It is very difficult to articulate certain complicated psychoanalytic complexes. In order to manage, I make use of the rigor of French, but the Spanish of Argentina provides me with its tempo and its very rhythmic melody. Thus, I benefit on all levels, from both rigor and musicality.

When did you learn about Lacan?
I learned of his name at the beginning of 1966, in a note at the bottom of the page of a book by Louis Althusser, a famous philosopher from the sixties. Interested in philosophy, I told myself, "What can this mean? A philosopher who reads a psychoanalyst named Lacan!" I immediately tried to find his books and by chance, I came across, a used copy of *Écrits* in a bookshop on Avenida Corrientes in Buenos Aires. I began to read him with a friend who knew French. Gradually, I arrived at the

idea that I should go to Paris to study Lacanian psychoanalysis at its
source. I managed to obtain a research grant from the French Embassy
in Buenos Aires for the purpose of developing my abilities in psychiatry
and psychoanalysis. Then, as soon as I arrived in Paris, I went directly
to visit Lacan. He was very moved to learn that the French government
had given a research grant to a young Argentinean psychiatrist to study
with him. Lacan was very sensitive to official recognition. This is how
our relationship began. After that, when he asked me to correct the
Spanish translation of *Écrits*, I had the opportunity to meet with him
quite often. We dined together frequently, and sometimes he even invited
me to his house in the country. I had the great privilege, being so young,
of working closely with him. Later, I was in supervision with him for
seven years and I joined his school. But the culminating event of our
relationship—an event that was for me an even greater honor than the
Légion d'Honneur (1999) and the *Ordre du Mérite* (2004)—took place the
morning of Monday, May 14, 1979, when Lacan said, "Nasio, tomorrow
you will give my seminar!" It was in this way that, deeply touched and
overcome by happiness and fear, I was to speak, standing at the same
pulpit from which the master usually spoke, before a huge audience
of eight hundred persons. This was, I can assure you, an exceptional
moment, and for me, even today, unforgettable.

Was Lacan as irascible as people claim?
Lacan was a very cordial, affable, and open man. But with him, one always
had the impression that there was a distance, even a certain reserve. When
one looked into Lacan's eyes, one could feel welcomed, but there was
a secret core that rendered him inaccessible. At the same time, he was
well aware of his intelligence and erudition. At times, he would adopt an
arrogant and a scornful tone toward certain persons, with the exception,
of course, of women. Yes, with women, Lacan always conducted himself
as a perfect gentleman, very attentive and even charming.

Was he short-tempered?
He was often irritated when his students could not understand his
thinking. Ignorance exasperated him. Moreover, he was irritated by the

idea that someone would copy him. He was very sensitive to plagiarism; not with respect to the plagiarism of his disciples, since, young as we were, we copied every detail, every comma, everything he said while trying to understand it in our own way. No, that did not bother him, but the venial plagiarism of his enemies triggered his anger.

Let's turn now to the theme of your book. What caused you to decide to write on the Oedipus complex?

On this theme, which is so fundamental, on such an overused psychoanalytic concept, unfortunate confusion prevails. Most people believe that the Oedipus complex is a love story: the little boy loves his mother and hates his father, with the inverse being true for the little girl. But, on the basis of my practice with children, and by studying the texts of the great founders of psychoanalysis, whether Freud, Melanie Klein, or Lacan, I learned clearly that the Oedipus complex has, above all, been a story of sexual desire and not of feelings. Freud's discovery was to have established that Oedipus is essentially a childhood experience of sexual desire. My personal interpretation is that it is a matter of an ardent desire, or a vivid erotic attachment of the child to the parents. The first idea that I would like to transmit to our American readers is that Oedipus is above all an erotic and sexual fire experienced by a four-year-old child in relation to his or her parents.

Is it this fire that you call "desire"?

Absolutely. To desire means to be in search of voluptuous sexual sensations that have already been experienced in the arms of the mother. Desire is a centrifugal movement toward the other. To what end? In order to speak with him or her? No. To seek tenderness? Even less. It is a movement toward the other to take hold of his or her body, to embrace it and draw pleasure from it. It is the physical pleasure of feeling his or her skin, of attracting his or her gaze, and to say it plainly, of feeling oneself engulfed by the fire of his or her desire. What is desire? Desire is the feverish search for pleasure in the physical exchange with the other. In this case, "exchange," does not simply mean to make love with him or her. To return to the Oedipal child, the child is inhabited by the desire to go toward the mother and to experience all the voluptuous sensations in contact with her body. In my practice, I received a three-year-old patient who told me that for him the greatest pleasure was to sleep in the bed next to his mother, to smell her and to feel comforted. I also think of that little girl who plays hobbyhorse with her father by balancing and swinging on his foot. Excited by the game, the little girl began to rub herself against the foot of her father. This is when, offended, he told her, "Hey, calm down, what are you doing there? If you continue we will stop!" This is the quite innocent sexual desire of a little girl who seeks to take pleasure in the physical contact with her father.

Why do you say that the Oedipus complex is psychoanalysis itself?
Because all of psychoanalysis and the psychoanalytic corpus, all of its concepts without exception, repression, sublimation, drive, desire, all these words that are part of the territory of psychoanalysis revolve around this idea that a three-year-old child desires to have physical pleasure with its parents, whether the pleasure of touching oneself, peeking, exhibiting oneself, or even the pleasure of hurting someone, biting or pinching. These desires are at the center of a major equation that constitutes the central axis of psychoanalysis: the human being is a being of desire. Instead of stating that Oedipus is psychoanalysis itself, I could have said that the conception that a psychoanalyst has of the human being corresponds exactly to the conception that he has of the Oedipal child. For we psychoanalysts, a human being is essentially an Oedipal child, that is to say:

A being of desire in relation to those who are near him or her and on whom he or she depends;
A being of fear since he or she is afraid of being punished for experiencing his or her desire and for trying to realize it;
And, finally, a being of fantasm who imagines the realization of forbidden desires, as well as the punishment that will follow.

In sum, the human being is a being of desire, of fear, and of fantasm. Now the Oedipal child is the most complete expression of the being that we are, of that being who feels his or her body burn from desire, who fears yielding to it, and whose solution to this desire/fear conflict is an imaginary staging of a scene of what would satisfy his or her desire.

How does a child make the transition from sexual desire to feelings of tenderness for his or her parents?

To be clear, tenderness already exists in interuterine life and expresses itself through different bodily movements of the fetus. Later, during the Oedipus complex, it coexists with sexual desire. However, the Oedipal child (from three to six years old) understands that the relation with his or her parents is complicated by the fact that they both excite and repress desire at the same time. Gradually, the little child manages to tame his or her desires and to live in society. This is what we all do. As adults, we experience our desires, our jealousies, our ambitions, our projects, and at the same time, we adapt ourselves to those around us. We learn that it is necessary for our desire to be tailored to the society in which we live. Do not forget that Oedipus is a crisis that is triggered at three years of age and is resolved at six years of age. In the beginning, the child thinks he or she can manifest his or her desire with impunity. Then, the child realizes that a compromise must be made between what he or she *wants* to do and what he or she *can* do. For example, the child learns that he or she cannot, at nine p.m. in the evening, leave its bed and parade nude before its parents who in the middle of having dinner with friends. If the child did this the parents would say, "But what are you doing there!? Get dressed and go back to bed!" Now from little transgressions such as this one, the child gradually discovers modesty and restraint. The Oedipal child is torn between four antagonistic drives: desire, of course, the feeling of tenderness toward the parents—tenderness that sublimates sexual desire—the feeling of the fear of transgressing prohibitions and being punished, and the feeling of rage against one's parents who prevent the child from expressing his or her desire. These antagonistic drives of desire, love, fear, and hate that are felt simultaneously constitute what is called a neurosis, a neurosis that causes suffering. Of course, this is a healthy developmental neurosis that lasts for the duration of the Oedipal crisis. Incontestably, this normal developmental neurosis, which affects children of all cultures, is a neurosis that can prolong itself in adult life. This depends in large part on the way in which the parents reacted to the Oedipal behavior of the children.

The little child desires to possess the other. Does the child desire to be possessed at the same time?

Your question leads me to distinguish between masculine and feminine desire. It is always difficult to define what is proper to masculinity and what is proper to femininity. In this book I did my best to propose a chart comparing the men's desire with the women's desires. I will summarize it for you here. The masculine desire is fundamentally a desire *to possess*, and feminine desire is fundamentally a desire *to be possessed*. I hasten to say to our American female readers that the desire to be possessed—eminently feminine—is in no way humiliating and does not in any way mean that the woman who experiences this desire feels, or is considered by her partner, as a passive or submissive object. No. The woman I am speaking about—proud of her identity as a woman, active and happy in the sexual relation—is a woman who undergoes *jouissance* from being possessed, and experiences the pleasure of penetration. This observation, drawn not only from the best textbooks of sexology, but also from the experience of my clinical practice, this observation holds true for the majority of women. We can find a great diversity in sexual behavior, but, for me, the desires that are the most characteristic of men and women are incontestably the masculine *desire to possess* and the feminine *desire to be possessed*. Having thus defined what is proper to men and to women, I have not forgotten that we are all fundamentally bisexual beings, and this is the case from the moment of our very gestation. The bisexuality to which I refer, however, is the bisexuality that is constitutive of the human being, a bisexuality that has nothing to do with the practice of bisexuality. It is one thing to affirm that as a human being I am bisexual, and quite another to declare that I make love with men and women indifferently. Let us therefore speak of a foundational bisexuality. A little girl, for example, around three years of age, during her Oedipal crisis, would like to possess her mother. For Freud, and for many other authors, this is described as a masculine attitude. The little Oedipal girl thus adopts a position that is somewhat aggressive, mean, authoritarian, and possessive toward her mother. In short, she adopts an eminently masculine position. Inversely, it happens also that a little boy, fundamentally animated by the desire to possess his mother, wants to be possessed, just like a little girl, by his father. These two types of desire, to possess and to be possessed, normally coexist in the boy and the girl, with a preponderance of the desire to possess in the case of the man and a preponderance of the desire to be possessed in the case of the woman. A man who feels quite virile can nevertheless express his feminine side, for example, by playing, during sexual activity, the role of an excited woman who offers herself to her partner.

Why do you say that a boy can leave Oedipus in a day and the girl only leaves after several years?
I meant that the boy is capable of renouncing the mother, fantasized as a sexual partner, in a day, while the girl is much slower to mourn the loss of her father. While the boy acquires his sexual identity through successive events, the girl acquires her sexual identity progressively without interruption. I would say that the tentative beginnings of the sexual identity of a human being begin already at the age of one and a half years. Certain American studies have shown that a child of one and a half years experiences masculine or feminine sensations. I believe this and I have also observed this in my consultations in Day Care facilities. However, with Oedipus, sexual identity will reinforce itself further.

For the boy, leaving Oedipus is therefore a moment that is clear and precise. Over the course of one or two years, he adopts an erotic attitude toward his mother, and then one day, he behaves completely differently, becoming exclusively modest and tender toward his mother. The little girl, for her part, will develop, with respect to her father, a seductive attitude that will last much longer. It is as if she would intimately nurture the hope of one day being possessed by the father. Even as an adolescent, she can be flirtatious with her father, or, on the contrary, enraged because he ignores her. A young boy in puberty is much more distant with his mother and less seductive.

*You say that the phallus of the man is power. What is the phallus
for the woman?*

The phallus of the woman is love. It is first necessary to explain what
the phallus is. Quite simply, it is the thing that one holds most dear.
For you, Professors Pettigrew and Raffoul, for example, as professors of
philosophy, the phallus is *thought* itself, the ability to think, to reflect,
and to transmit your knowledge to young students. This work of
conceptualization and teaching causes you, no doubt, to suffer, but it
also gives you much satisfaction. Perhaps, at times, you ask yourselves
whether or not you should continue in this career. There is no need to
be a psychoanalyst in order to realize that within you, the exercise of
thought is a practice you do not wish to renounce. This is because
you have wanted to do this since your adolescence, and because
you are among the pioneers in the United States in the field of
French philosophy and psychoanalysis. You have created a domain of
intellectual inquiry that did not exist. I am sure that this is what you
hold most dear and what you fear losing. This is what one calls a phallus!
If you lose it you will be quite affected and hurt! A phallus is what
we all hold most dear: you, I, or the reader, who reads this at this very
moment. If one day we lose this precious thing, we will feel the pain of
a mourning.

If the woman's phallus is essentially love, that is, the fact of loving and
being loved, for the man it is essentially his power, the power of being
able to do what he has to do.

*One last question: Why do you write that men are cowards
and women are dreamers?*

I do think that men are cowards and women are dreamers. Men are
cowards because they are so concerned with their power, strength, and
virility that they are always afraid of losing them. Hence, they accomplish actions and make decisions in their lives that are always destined
to protect, to protect their power and potentialities, to protect what
they consider to be most vital in their existence, beginning with their
self-image, and pride of being men. In this way, men are extremely
fearful, insofar as they are permanently exposed and imagine having

everything to lose. For their part, women are clearly more coura-
geous than men are. Women certainly have their fears, but they have
nothing to lose, because in their early childhood, they had already gone
through the experience of loss. While they decide to confront whatever
difficulty, they know that they are not risking everything, and they go
forward without hesitation. We men, however, on the contrary imagine
that we might lose everything. This is how fear and doubt consume us.
We say more easily than women, "I do not know, let us wait, let me see."
We tremble, and deliberate endlessly. We have, no doubt, other qualities,
but being cowardly is our most vulnerable feature, our Achilles heel.
Thank you, Dr. Nasio.

No Child Escapes Oedipus!

The Oedipus I will address in this book is a legend that provides an account of the origin of our sexual identity as a man or as a woman and, moreover, the origin of our neurotic suffering. This legend concerns all children, whether they live in a traditional family, with a single parent, in a family composed of previously divorced parents, whether they grow up with homosexual parents, or whether they are abandoned, orphans, or wards of the state. No child escapes Oedipus! Why? Because no four-year-old child, boy or girl, escapes the flood of erotic drives that surges through them, and because no adult in his or her immediate surroundings can avoid being the target of these drives and of having to resist [*endiguer*] them.

Introduction

A child's intercourse with anyone responsible for his care affords him an unending source of sexual excitation and satisfaction from his erotogenic zones. This is especially so since the person in charge of him, who, after all, is as a rule his mother, herself regards him with feelings that are derived from her own sexual life: she strokes him, kisses him, rocks him and quite clearly treats him as a substitute for a complete sexual object. A mother would probably be horrified if she were made aware that all her marks of affection were rousing the child's sexual instinct and preparing for its later intensity. She regards what she does as asexual, "pure" love, since, after all, she carefully avoids applying more excitations to the child's genitals than are unavoidable in nursery care. As we know, however, the sexual instinct is not aroused only by direct excitation of the genital zone. What we call affection will unfailingly show its effects one day on the genital zones as well.

—*Freud, "Three Essays on the Theory of Sexuality."*

"The boy is in love with his mother and wants to get rid of his father; the daughter, for her part, is in love with her father, and wants to get rid of her mother." Here, in a few words, is the oldest cliché of psychoanalysis, the most celebrated love-drama: the Oedipus complex. And nevertheless, nothing is more deceptive than this standard account of the Freudian complex. Why? Because the Oedipus complex is not a story of love or hate between parents and children. It is a story of sex, that is to say, a story of bodies that take pleasure from caressing, kissing, and biting each other, exhibiting themselves and looking at each other, in short, of bodies that take as much pleasure from touching themselves as they

1

do from hurting themselves. No. Oedipus is not a matter of feeling and tenderness, but rather concerns bodies of desire, fantasies and pleasure. No doubt, parents and children love each other tenderly and can hate each other, but at the heart of the love and the hate of the family, sexual desire simmers.

Oedipus entails an immense excess: it is a sexual desire proper to an adult, experienced in the immature body and mind of a four-year-old child, whose parents are the object of that desire. The Oedipal child is a joyous child who, in all innocence, sexualizes his parents, includes them in his fantasies as objects of desire, and mimics their sexual gestures without shame or moral sense. It is the first time in his life that the child experiences an erotic movement of his entire body toward the body of an other. It is no longer a question of a mouth that seeks a breast but of an entire being that wants to embrace the entire body of his mother. Now, if it is true that the Oedipal child is happy to desire, and with the pleasure derived from it, it is even more true that desire and pleasure frighten him because he fears them as a danger. What danger? The danger of seeing his body overcome by the ardor of his passion; the danger of seeing his head explode due to the failure to master his desire mentally; and finally, the danger of being punished by the Law of the prohibition of incest, for having taken his parents as sexual partners. Excited by his desire, happy with his fantasies but also anguished, the child is lost and completely bewildered. The Oedipal crisis is an unbearable conflict between erotic pleasure and fear, between the exaltation of desire and the fear of disappearing in the flames of desire.

Thus, the child reacts without compromise. Torn between joy and anxiety, there is no other way out than by forgetting and erasing everything. Yes, the Oedipal child, whether boy or girl, vigorously represses fantasies and anxiety, ceases to take his or her parents as sexual partners, and becomes, from then on, free to conquer new and legitimate objects of desire. It is in this way that the child progressively discovers shame, develops the feeling of guilt, and moral sense, and determines his or her sexual identity as male or female. Let us note that after a period of relative calm with respect to the drives—and I do mean relative—puberty brings about a second Oedipal shock. Just as he had already done at four years of age, the young adolescent will have to adapt the ardor of his or her impulses to his or her new body, which is in full pubescent metamorphosis, and to new social demands. But such an adjustment is never easy for a youngster and this is why we find so many difficulties with an adolescent in crisis. The young person no longer knows how to alleviate his or her drives as he or she had done at the end of the Oedipus stage; on the contrary, he or she stokes his or her desire by rebelling, and sometimes, on the contrary, he or she suppresses his desire so brutally that he or she becomes inhibited and quite withdrawn. Nevertheless, the Oedipal volcano does not extinguish itself in adolescence. Much later, in adulthood, on the occasion of an emotional conflict, new eruptive episodes can break out in the form of neurotic disorders such as phobia, hysteria, and obsession. Finally, let us not forget that another reactivation of Oedipus can come up, this time experimentally, in the psychoanalytic scene at the heart of the transference neurosis. I will state this in the following formulation: the transference between the patient and the analyst is the repetition, in act, of the Oedipus complex.

What then is Oedipus? Oedipus is the experience undergone by a child around four years of age who, overcome by an uncontrollable sexual desire, must learn to control his or her drives and adjust them to the limits of his or her immature body, emerging consciousness, fear, and finally to the limits of a tacit Law that orders him or her to stop treating his or her parents as sexual objects. This is what is essential in the Oedipal crisis: to learn to channel an excessive desire. With respect to Oedipus, it is the first time in our lives that we say to our insolent desire: "Calm down! Behave yourself! Learn to live in society!" Thus, we conclude that Oedipus is the painful rite of passage of a wild desire into a socialized desire and the acceptance—which is just as painful—that our desires can never be completely satisfied.

Oedipus, however, is not only a sexual crisis related to maturation; it is also the fantasm that this crisis forms in the infantile unconscious. In fact, the lived experience of the Oedipal seism is registered in the unconscious of the child and perdures until the end of his or her life as a fantasm that will define the sexual identity of the subject, will determine numerous features of its personality, and will establish its aptitude to resolve affective conflicts. In the case where the child would have experienced, during the Oedipal crisis, a pleasure that was too precocious, intense, and unexpected, that is to say, in the case where the experience of an excessive pleasure was traumatic, the resulting fantasm would be the certain cause of a future neurosis.

However, Oedipus is more than a sexual crisis and the fantasm that it forms in the unconscious; it is also a concept, the most crucial of psychoanalytic concepts. I would say that it is psychoanalysis itself, since the entirety of the sensations that a child undergoes during this sexual experience we call the Oedipus complex, is, for us psychoanalysts, the model that allows us to understand the adult that we are. Like the Oedipal child, we experience the rising of our desire toward the other, we form fantasies, we take pleasure with our own bodies or with the body of the other person, we fear being overcome by our drives, and we learn, finally, to restrain our desire and our pleasure in order to live in society. What is psychoanalysis if not a practice sustained by a theory that conceives of human beings today on the basis of the Oedipal trial that all children undergo when they must learn to restrain their desire and temper their pleasure?

Finally, Oedipus is also a myth, since this real and concrete crisis that survives in a four-year-old child, this crisis is a devastating allegory of combat between impetuous forces of individual desire and the forces of the civilization that opposes them. The best way out of this conflict is a compromise that entails *modesty* and *intimacy*.

What is the status of Oedipus? A Reality, a Fantasm, a Concept, or a Myth?

What then is the true status of Oedipus? Is it a sexual crisis related to maturation that can be observed in the behavior of children? Is it a fantasm inscribed in the unconscious? Or is it rather the most important theoretical construction, the keystone of the analytic edifice? Or is it simply a myth, the modern myth that reveals that the universal prohibition of incest is a response to the mad incestuous human desire. Is Oedipus, then, a reality, a fantasm, a concept, or quite simply a myth?

I would respond that Oedipus is all of them: reality, fantasm, concept, and myth. Nevertheless, for psychoanalysts, Oedipus remains above all a fantasm, I should say, a double fantasm. It is the infantile fantasm active in the unconscious of the adult patient that is reconstructed by the practitioner in analysis. I can only understand the suffering of my adult patients in terms of the desires, fictions and anxieties they experienced at the Oedipal stage. And I tell myself that these infantile desires, fictions, and anxieties are still present today, disguised in the numerous agonies of the patients' neuroses. When, for example, I listen to "Sarah," a twenty-six-year-old who is severely anorexic, in my mind I see the little girl that she was and I imagine how she was torn between the desire to be a boy with a "flat" body like that of her brother, the favorite child of the father, and the desire of being the women loved by the father. Now, it is by addressing myself to this little four-year-old girl within Sarah that I can have a chance of influencing the course of her anorexia. When, during a session, I suggest an interpretation, it is Sarah the patient who hears it, but it is the little Sarah who receives it. Which little Sarah? She is the little Oedipal girl that I imagine in my listening and that I suppose to be active in the unconscious of the adult Sarah. But what proves that this fantasm, forged in the listening with the aid of the clinical material and Oedipal theory, is indeed the one that acts in the unconscious of my patient? What guarantees that the fantasm, in which the little Sarah is torn between the desire to be a boy and that of being a woman, is not an erroneous construction? In other words, what is the validity of this fantasm and of the Oedipal concept that subtends it? I would suggest that this concept and this fantasm are valid for two essential reasons. First, because each time I listen to a patient with the theoretical *a priori* of Oedipus and the fantasm that it entails, my intervention turn out to be pertinent, that is to say that they are validated thereafter by the very patient. Second, and, finally, because I have the confirmation through my experience that the listening, enriched by the concept of Oedipus, is an extremely supple, malleable listening that is capable of harmonizing the present occurrence of the suffering of the patient, the fantasm of the child that he or she was, and the rigor of a psychoanalytical theory that I constantly fashion and appropriate in my work.

★   ★   ★

If now I were to schematize the Oedipal crisis in two main stages, I would say that Oedipus begins with the *sexualization* of the parents and ends with their *desexualization*, a desexualization that leads finally to adult sexual identity.

I would like to present in detail, in what follows, the logic of the Oedipal crisis for the boy and for the girl, using a metapsychological legend and narrative that I have forged in the light of psychoanalytic theory and on the basis of my clinical experience. But first it is necessary to indicate the main elements of the crisis: *incestuous desires, fantasms,* and *identification.* We will first address the incestuous desires; then we will consider the three main fantasms of the Oedipus complex: fantasms of *phallic* omnipotence—the child believes itself to be omnipotent; fantasms of *pleasure* that provide the imaginary satisfaction of incestuous desire—the child is joyful; fantasms of *anxiety* in the case of the boy—the boy is fearful—and fantasms of *pain* in the case of the girl—the little girl is battered; and finally, the last link of the Oedipal logic, the surprising phenomenon of *identification.* Desires, fantasms and identification are thus the three operators that punctuate respectively the birth, apogee and decline of the Oedipus complex (Diagram 1).

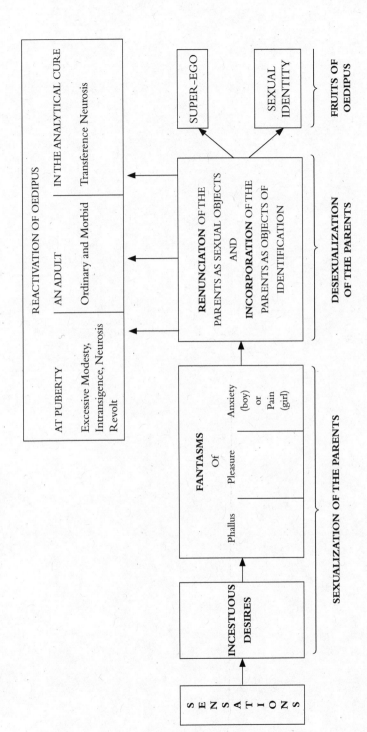

Diagram 1 General View of Oedipus

The Oedipus of the Boy

In the Beginning Was the Body of Erogenous Sensations

The Three Incestuous Desires

The Three Fantasms of Pleasure

The Three Fantasms of Castration Anxiety

The Resolution of the Boy's Oedipus Complex:
The Desexualization of the Parents

Compared to Women, Men Are Essentially Cowards

The Fruits of the Oedipus Complex: The Super-Ego
and Sexual Identity

Summary of the Logic of the Boy's Oedipus

In the Beginning Was the Body of Erogenous Sensations

(This section is to be read with conjunction with Diagram 2 on page 26.)

Around three or four years of age, all boys focus their pleasure on the penis, as an organ, an imaginary object and as a symbolic emblem. At that age, the penile organ becomes the part of the body that is richest in sensations and imposes itself as the dominant erogenous zone because the pleasure it gives the child becomes the principal reference for all other corporeal pleasures. Before that age, the sites of pleasure were the mouth, the anus, and muscular activity—let us not forget the pleasure of walking, running, and acting prevails in the lives all children between the ages of two and three—while thereafter at four years of age, all corporeal pleasure, whatever zone is excited, registers in his little penis in the form of a quiver of pleasure. In other words, if a four-year-old boy enjoys looking at the mother's cleavage or enjoys exhibiting himself in public, or, if excited by the game, he bites his little sister's thigh, we would say that all these pleasures, gained from the excitation of the eyes, the teeth, or the body as a whole, are all pleasures that register in his little sex and already cause him to experience genital excitation.

But when the boy is four years old, the penis is not only the most sensitive organ, it is also the most cherished object and the one that demands all the attention. A visible appendage, easily manipulated, erogenous and erectile, the penis attracts the hand, just as the nipple attracts the lips and the tongue; the penis attracts looks, arouses the curiosity of boys and girls, and inspires their fables, stories, and bizarre sexual theories. The imaginary fullness [*prégnance*] of the penis is such that the boy makes it his most precious narcissistic object, the thing he is most attached to and that he is proud to possess. Consequently, such penis worship raises the little organ to a symbol of absolute power and the emblem of virile force. A cautionary note: it is also, and for the same reasons, experienced as fragile organ, overexposed to dangers and, thus, not only a symbol of power, but also a symbol of vulnerability and weakness. When such an erectile, easily manipulated, eminently excitable, clearly visible, and highly valued appendage becomes in everyone's eyes—both boys and girls—a representative of desire, we call it the "Phallus." The Phallus is not the penis in the sense of being an organ. The Phallus is the fantasmatic, idealized penis, a symbol of omnipotence and, inversely, of vulnerability. We will see further when we approach the feminine Oedipus in detail that the imaginary and symbolic prevalence of the penis is so strong at this age that the little girl will believe that she also possesses a Phallus. It is precisely the penis fantasized as a Phallus that lends its name to the phase of the libidinal development during which the Oedipal crisis arises. Freud calls this stage, when infantile sexuality remains centered on the Phallus, *the phallic stage* (pp. 51–52).

During this stage, children—whether boys or girls—believe that all beings in the world are endowed with a powerful Phallus, that is to say, that all human beings are as strong as they are. When, for example, a boy tells himself that everyone in the world has a Phallus, he thinks: "Everyone in the world possesses a penile organ like mine. Everyone has the same sensations I do and everyone must feel as strong as I do." I emphasize that this infantile fiction, this illusion that the penis is a universal attribute, is concocted as much by the boy as by the girl. Now the idolatry of the child for the Phallus will be accompanied by the little boy's anxiety of losing it and by the little girl's pain of having lost it. In fact, at this age, the child has already had the experience of losing vital objects; as a baby the child has lost the maternal breast that it considered to be part of itself; the child has then gone through the experience of renouncing the pacifier and of separating itself from its first "cuddly toy"; and later, the experience of going to the toilet and of observing its first "poop" leave it. It has also had the experience of losing its privileged status with the birth of a little brother or sister; and finally, it has perhaps already experienced the death of a loved one who was close. In sum, at the Oedipal age, the child can perfectly well conceive of the loss of a cherished object and fear being unable to reproduce it. However, in order to be more precise, I should add that ever since coming to the world, ever since the first palpitations of its embryonic body, the little human being is already perfectly capable of feeling the lack of a vital object. I would even say it is capable of feeling lack itself. We know how a baby, as little as it is, feels, knows, and cries from pain when it lacks something essential. This is why I would say that the Oedipal child's aptitude for representing the lack is, in the end, an intuition inherent to the human species.

But let us return to our discussion. Recall the remark concerning the fiction of a universal Phallus and of the capacity of a young child to intuitively represent a lack to itself. These two propositions are indispensable premises for understanding how the fantasm of castration *anxiety* in the boy and the *pain* of privation in the girl is formed, that is to say, to understand how the boy overcomes Oedipus and how the girl enters it. We will return to this later.

Three Incestuous Desires

Let us consider, first, the dynamic of incestuous desires. Sexually excited and proud of his power, the little four-year-old boy perceives a new force emerging within himself, an unknown *élan*: the desire to go toward the Other, to go toward his parents, and more exactly, to go toward the body of his parents in order to find pleasure there, that is, to find the entirety of erogenous pleasures known before this age. This is the novelty of Oedipus! Up to this stage, the child had not known such a blooming of the senses and had not experienced such an ardent desire to possess the entire body of the Other and to find pleasure therein. What is desire? Desire is the *élan* that pushes us to seek pleasure in the embrace with our partner. One always desires a person in the flesh [*une personne dans sa chair*]. To desire is to throw oneself outside of the self in quest of the flesh of the other. It is to wish to attain, through the flesh, and by the flesh, the most exquisite *jouissance*. This is desire! This is how any desire is a sexual desire. *Sexual* means more than *genital*. Sexual means: "Let me see your body nude! Caress it, feel it, kiss it, devour it, and even destroy it!" What bodies? The bodies of those that I love who attract me and who are within reach. And who are those for a child if not the mother and the father? Like a mischievous kitten, the Oedipal child cuts his teeth of desire on the backs of his parents. The Oedipal child, then, is caught up in an impulse that pushes it and compels it to seek its pleasure in the sensual exchange with the bodies of those it loves, on whom it depends, and who are also desiring beings, beings who call for and maintain its desire. Now this imperious desire, this irresistible *élan* whose source is penile excitations, whose end is pleasure, and whose object is the body of one of the genitors or any other adult figure, this *élan* is an expression of the mythical desire of incest. Yes, Oedipus is the infantile attempt to realize an incestuous desire than cannot be realized. But what is **incestuous desire**? It is a *virtual desire, never satisfied, whose object is one of the parents and whose aim would not be physical plea-sure but* **jouissance**. What *jouissance*? The prodigious *jouissance* derived from a perfect sexual relation where the two partners, child and adult, would disappear in a total and ecstatic fusion. Of course, this desire is a dream that cannot be realized, a marvelous fantasy, the Greek myth or the wildest and immemorial fables. I will immediately clarify that the genuine father/daughter or father/son incestuous acting out, and more rarely between mother/son, are relatively uncommon transgres-sions, and when they do occur they never provide *jouissance* whether prodigious or banal. Nothing of the kind! On the contrary, with respect to incestuous cases, clinical experience proves the extreme poverty of the satisfaction obtained by the perverse adult and the deep trauma experienced by the child. No. The incestuous desire of which we speak has nothing in common with the misery of sexual abuse of a child by the father. But you will ask why psychoanalysis has the need to regard incestuous desire as sacred and to postulate that all desires, however insignificant, refer to a virtual desire as well? Why is incestuous desire the standard? The only value of this mad desire to sleep with one's mother and to kill one's father is that it serves as the allegory of the demented desire for a return to the original state of intrauterine bliss. For psychoanalysis, each of our everyday desires—the sensual pleasure of contemplating a painting or that of caressing the body of a loved one, for example—each of these desires, I insist, would tend, from a theoretical point of view, toward the perfect happiness that two persons becoming One would enjoy. Incestuous desire, then, is only a mythical figure of the absolute, the mad desire of a hero who penetrates his mother in order to retrieve his origin deep within the maternal body. To express it in an image, incestuous desire is the desire of fusion with our nourishing source.

Once we recognize the mythical character of incestuous desire, I would distinguish three variations of it in the boy. Let us emphasize already that the incestuous desires are not exclusively erotic but rather a concentration of erotic and aggressive tendencies. Hence, there are three fundamental desires present in a boy and present in any humans who are masculine, whatever their age: the *desire to possess* the body of the Other sexually, in particular the mother; the *desire to be possessed* by the body of the Other, in particular by the father; and the *desire of suppressing the body* of the Other, in particular of the father. The desire to *possess*, the desire to *be possessed*, and the desire of *suppressing*; these are the three fundamental movements of masculine desire.

The Three Fantasms of Pleasure

Now, the failure to attain these three incestuous and impossible goals—to attain the absolute *jouissance* of possessing the body of the Other, to be possessed by the Other, that is to say, to be its thing and to give it *jouissance*; and finally to attain the absolute *jouissance* of suppressing the Other—the little boy invents fantasms that give him pleasure or anxiety but which in any case satisfy, in an imaginary sense, his mad desires.

But what is a fantasm? It is a scene, usually unconscious, destined to satisfy, in an imaginary manner, the incestuous desire that cannot be realized, or rather to satisfy any desire since all desire is an expression of incestuous desire. A fantasm is an imaginary scene that brings the child some relief, and this relief takes the form of a pleasure, or as we will see, the form of an anxiety. Hence, the function of the fantasm is to replace an ideal action that would bring an inhuman *jouissance* through a fantasized action that diminishes the tension of the desire and provides pleasure, anxiety, or still other feelings that are at times painful. In fact, the diminution of the psychical tension through the fantasm does not always result in an agreeable relief, but quite often it results in troubles and torments that, as painful as they are, prevent an irreparable psychical break from occurring. As surprising as this may seem, the diminution of psychical tension can also result in conscious suffering. A tearful breakdown, for example, can play the role of a salutary discharge, or, an incapacitating phobic symptom can appear as a lesser evil that protects someone from something more serious, such as a psychosis.

Let us note further that the scene of the fantasm is not necessarily conscious and often results in the everyday life of the child in a feeling—as we have just seen—an attitude or a comment. A little boy can never have a sexual relation with his mother, but he will compensate for this impossibility through a voyeuristic fantasm in which he imagines her nude. This fantasm will present itself through the mischievous wish to spy on and surprise his mother in intimate situations. We have here the stages I referred to previously: the incestuous desire of possessing the mother, the desire derived from seeing the nude body of the mother, the fantasm of imagining it, and finally the mischievous gesture of looking through the keyhole, a gesture that activates the fantasm.

I would like however, to dissipate any confusion concerning the following terms: "feelings, desires, fantasms, and behavior." Let us be clear. First, sensations awaken the desire of going toward the body of the adult. Then this desire is satisfied through fantasms that give the child pleasure. I would like to repeat that these fantasms of pleasure are rarely visualized mentally by the subject. It is we psychoanalysts who deduce them from our observations of childhood behavior and above all from listening to our adult patients. We listen to a patient, a child or an adult, and we reconstruct the fantasmatic scenes that govern their lives. In a more abstract way, we can say that these scenes are forged *unconsciously* by the subject in order to achieve an imaginary satisfaction of his desire—a desire that is, in our example, voyeuristic—and beyond that, to satisfy his mythical desire of incest. If I learn that a little boy is spying on his mother, then I deduce that he is unconsciously animated by a voyeuristic scene in which his mother is nude. I also tell myself that this scene satisfies the incestuous desire to possess his mother, and more concretely, the desire to devour her with his eyes. *In sum, the sensations awaken the desire, the desire calls forth the fantasm, and the fantasm is actualized through a feeling, a behavior, or a speech.* Also, when you are faced with an emotion, you can say that it expresses a fantasm and that the fantasm satisfies a desire, a desire that is always revivified by the body of sensations.

Having made these clarifications, we can see now how the three incestuous desires are satisfied in an imaginary way, due to a particular fantasm of pleasure. A specific fantasm of pleasure corresponds to each incestuous desire. What, then, is the fantasm that is specific to the incestuous desire of *possessing the Other*? In fact, this fantasm assumes several forms in which the child always plays an active role, and feels proud to impose his presence on the Other. The fantasm of possession is manifest through behavior typical of that age, such as exhibiting oneself in a shameless way, playing "mommy and daddy," playing doctor, playing the clown, using foul language, or even mimicking sexual postures. Sometimes the main activity consists in touching the body of one of his parents, or his brothers, or sisters, or kissing it feverishly, or biting or mistreating it. But of all the scenarios of possession, the one that most faithfully expresses the incestuous desire of possessing the Other is the wish of the boy to monopolize his mother and have her all for himself.

I would like to give you an example. I am thinking of a three-year-old boy named Martin. He is a lively boy, as mischievous as they come. His mother, one of my analysands, brought him to my office one day, since she had no one to watch him. While the child played in the waiting room next to my office the mother told me an anecdote about her son, as if in confidence, that I took to be a beautiful illustration of a fantasm of the Oedipal pleasure of possessing the mother. Martin's mother is a very pretty young divorcée with a pleasant demeanor, who lives alone with the child. Here is what she confided to me: "Guess what happened to me Doctor, with Martin, the little devil. I was in the bathroom, barely dressed, putting on my makeup—I always leave the door slightly ajar—when suddenly I screamed: Martin had entered silently, on tiptoe, and had bitten my buttocks, and then ran away quite proud and happy with what he had done." I ask you to imagine this little boy slipping into the bathroom and discovering, at eye level, the appealing buttocks of his mother. With a twinkle in the eye, he approached, and without any warning, he took a big bite. This . . . is Oedipus! *Oedipus* means, to bite the mother's buttocks! Oedipus is not to tenderly caress one's mother, but to desire and bite her. It seems obvious now that I discuss this with you, but this revelation of the sexual nature of Oedipus, namely, that Oedipus involves sex and not love, is something that is not always recognized. Oedipus is the sexual desire of a little boy who has neither the mental nor physical maturity to handle it.

After this first Oedipal fantasm of possessing the mother, we come to the second fantasm of pleasure, that of *being possessed by the Other*. The most typical fantasm of the desire of being possessed is a scene where the boy takes pleasure in seducing an adult in order to become its object. This fantasm is a fantasm of sexual seduction in which the seducing boy imagines being seduced by his mother, by his older brother, or even, as surprising as it may seem, by his own father. In fact, the boy can play a passive, eminently feminine role, of being the thing of his father, and giving him pleasure. But it is necessary to understand that, if the child imagines being seduced, he is not only the passive victim of a perverse, evil, or abusive father, the child is also an active seducer who expects to be seduced. The child seduces in order to be seduced. Let us note that if this Oedipal fantasm of the seduction of the boy by the father hardens and later invades the life of the adult that the child has become, it acts as a noxious agent, the frequent cause of a form of masculine hysteria that is very difficult to treat. Often the psychoanalytic treatment of this hysteria fails and ends on a crisis called "the rock of castration," or as Adler referred to it, "virile protestation." Since we are referring to the clinical experience, I would like to stress that my choice to address the Oedipus complex is due to the fact that I would like enrich psychoanalytic practice with adult patients. For, the interest of the Oedipus complex is not only theoretical, but above all clinical, as the fantasm of seduction is a patent illustration of it. Each time that I receive neurotic men who ask me for an analysis, I think of their unconscious fantasm of being the thing of the father and of giving him pleasure [*et de le faire jouir*].

The last fantasm of pleasure, the one of the desire *to suppress the Other*, in particular the father, places the subject in an active sexual position. I say "sexual" because to destroy the Other provokes as much sexual pleasure as any Oedipal fantasm. One of the childhood comportments that best expresses the fantasm of making the rival father disappear, is the common one in which the little boy takes advantage of the father's absence, who may be traveling, to play the role as the "the man of the house," and, for example, to want to share the conjugal bed with the mother.

The Three Fantasms of Castration Anxiety

The fantasms of *pleasure*, whether the one where the boy adopts an active sexual posture such as when he bites the mother; or the one where the boy adopts a passive sexual attitude such as seducing in order to be seduced; or finally the one where he adopts the active sexual posture of rejecting the father; all these fantasms are fantasms of pleasure that make the child happy but which also trigger in him a profound *anxiety*: the mischievous little boy fears being punished where he has sinned, punished by the mutilation of his virile organ, the symbol of his power, his pride, and his pleasure. This fantasm in which he would be punished by the mutilation of his Phallus is called the fantasm of "castration anxiety." Let us be clear. The threat of being punished by castration and the anxiety that it provokes are a threat and an anxiety that are *fantasmatic*. Certainly a boy can commit a misdeed and be in fear of being chastised, but the fantasm of being punished by castration and the anxiety which result from it are unconscious. The anxiety of castration is not felt by the boy, for it is unconscious. This is an important point because many practitioners would like to verify if a four-year-old little boy actually fears the mutilation of his penis. And I would say immediately that without exception there will never be any confirmation of such a fear. Certainly it often happens that a mother, seeing her son touch his sex will shout: "Stop playing with it. Your little bird is not going to fly away and no one will eat it." But this is a remark that will hardly provoke castration anxiety in the little boy. No, castration anxiety is never conscious. That being the case, how are we to consider the anxieties that we observe everyday in children in the guise of fears or nightmares. I would say that these childhood anxieties are the clinical forms assumed by unconscious castration anxiety. In sum, it matters little whether a boy faces a real threat and becomes anxious. What matters is that in any case the child is inhabited by unconscious castration anxiety. As long as he desires and gains pleasure, however minimal, he will be anxious. Anxiety is the inverse [*l'envers*] of pleasure. Anxiety and pleasure are so indistinguishable that I imagine them as twins of desire. Let me be clear on this point: in the same way that psychoanalysis postulates the premise of incestuous desire, it affirms that all men are essentially inhabited by a castration anxiety that is intrinsic to their masculine desire. We will return to this later when we address masculine neurosis, but I already assert now that castration anxiety is the backbone of the male psyche. We will return later to the question of the emotional psyche of the woman.

Hence, masculine anxiety is the reverse side of fantasmatic pleasure. In fact, there is no Oedipal pleasure without its counterpart: the anxiety of desire and of being punished. This couple of antagonistic feelings, pleasure and the fear of being punished, is at the basis of any neurosis. One can say at the outset that Oedipus itself is a childhood neurosis, or better yet, the first neurosis related to the development of the human being. Why? It is because this neurosis is, above all, the simultaneous action of opposite feelings and because the Oedipal child, like the neurotic person, suffers from a painful tension between the enjoyment of the pleasure of the fantasm and the fear of punishment if it perseveres. I will return later and often to this cardinal idea that Oedipus is in itself a neurosis.

Although we have already posited the unconscious status of castration anxiety without having justified it with concrete situations, it is no less apparent that certain incidents of the life of the child confirm, if need be, the existence of this anxiety. Here is the incontrovertible event to which all theoretical discussions of Oedipus refer. One day, the boy sees the nude body of a little girl, or of his own mother, and observes, in surprise, that they do not have a penis-Phallus. If we recall the childhood illusion according to which the whole world possesses the Phallus we can understand that the boy tells himself unconsciously: "Since there is someone in this world who has lost his or her Phallus, I also risk being deprived of mine." It is with this discovery that castration anxiety is definitively confirmed.

We have then three variations of the fantasm of anxiety that have to
be understood as the reverse side of the three fantasms of pleasure:

- If the fantasm of pleasure is to bite the mother or to have a child
  with her, that is to say, *to possess the Other*, castration anxiety concerns
  the most precious object, the *penis-Phallus*, that is to say, the part of
  the body that is most invested. Here the *agent* of the threat is the
  prohibiting father who reminds the child of the law of the prohibition
  of incest: "You cannot possess your mother nor give her a child!"
  Also, he addresses himself to the mother and says: *"You cannot nurse
  your child again!"*
- If the fantasm of pleasure is a fantasm of seduction, that is to say,
  of *being possessed by the Other*, more precisely, of offering oneself to
  the father, castration anxiety equally concerns the Phallus, but in
  this case considered less as a detachable appendage than as a symbol
  of virility. Here the *agent* of the threat is not the prohibiting father,
  but the *seductive father*. The father is a lover that the boy desires,
  but fears that he might go too far and abuse him. In this case the
  anxiety is not the fear of losing his penis-Phallus but of losing his
  virility by becoming the female-object of the father. "I fear being
  abused sexually by my father and losing my virility." I insist that the
  fantasm of the seduction of the boy by the father and the anxiety
  of being abused is a primordial fantasm that must be recognized in
  the analytic cure of neurotic males.
- Finally, if the fantasm of pleasure is a fantasm of getting rid of the
  father as rival, castration anxiety bears again on the penis-Phallus
  considered as the exposed part of the body. Here the *agent* of the
  threat is the hated father who intimidates the child in order to stop
  his parricidic impulses.

These, then, are the three variations of the fantasm of castration
anxiety. In the first, the father is the prohibitor that one fears. In the
second, the father is an abuser that one fears. In the third, the father is a
rival that one fears. In all three cases the agent of the threat is the father
and the object threatened is the penis-Phallus, or its derivation, virility.

The Resolution of the Boy's Oedipus Complex: The Desexualization of the Parents

The boy renounces his mother because he fears being punished in his flesh, while the girl—as we will see—leaves her mother who disappoints her and turns toward the father.

Where does castration anxiety lead us? Well, it is that very anxiety that precipitates the end of the Oedipal crisis. In fact, torn between the fantasms of pleasure and the fantasms of anxiety, divided between joy and fear, the boy is finally overcome by fear. Anxiety, stronger than pleasure, dissuades the child from pursing his incestuous quest and leads him to *renounce* the object of his desires. Anxiety-ridden, the child avoids his parents as sexual objects in order to save his precious penis-Phallus, that is to say, to protect his body. The Oedipus complex culminates and comes to an end, with the renunciation of the parents and the submission to the law of the prohibition of incest. Finally, the child succeeds in preserving his Phallus but at the price of abandoning his sexualized parents. We can say this in another way. Facing the threat, the anxiety-ridden boy must choose between keeping his mother or keeping his penis. Thus, it is his penis that he will keep and his mother that he will relinquish. By renouncing the mother, he desexualizes both parents and represses desires, fantasms, and anxiety. Relieved, he can now remain open to other desirable but now legitimate objects that are realistic possibilities. It is only in this way, when he is sexually detached from his parents, that the child can henceforth desire other partners outside the family.

Compared to Women Men, are Essentially Cowards

As the son is loved by his mother so he becomes a virile man. And as he will be proud of his power, so he will be careful to defend it, susceptible with respect to his virility and ridiculously sensitive to the least injury. Compared to women, men are essentially cowards.

I would like to outline the sequence of the Oedipal crisis of the boy. We have then, three stages: *Love of the penis* => *Anxiety of losing it* =>*Renunciation of the mother.* Because of the anxiety, the narcissism of the boy, that is to say his love for his own body, the love for his penis-Phallus, prevails over the desire for his parents. Faced with the threat, the narcissism is stronger than the desire, in other words, the drive to self-preservation overcomes the sexual drives. I want to emphasize that this victory of narcissism over desire is precipitated by anxiety: do not forget that it is due the fear of being hurt that the boy abandons his mother. However, the anxiety is repressed, and often badly repressed. In fact, we will see that the adult neurosis is the return of castration anxiety that was poorly repressed in childhood. But in addition to this neurotic return, it is incontestable that castration anxiety remains omnipresent in the normal relations that a man maintains with his genitals organs and, more generally, with his virility. Despite its repression by the Oedipal child, anxiety, the pivot of the Oedipus of the boy, always determines the masculine condition. We can then deduce how anxiety is at the center of the life of a man. It permeates the masculine character so thoroughly that I would not hesitate to say, and analytic experience proves it, that man is particularly fearful when faced with physical pain and concerned to assure the permanence of his virility and his power. Man is *par essence* a being who is anxious about losing the power he believes that he possesses or, to say it dramatically, man is a coward. Yes, I recognize it, we men are cowards to the core, and this cowardice comes from fear. The fear comes from the excessive narcissism of the body, and the anxious and nervous attention we pay to our own body, specifically, the attention that we pay, not to the appearance or beauty of the body, but to its vigor and above all its integrity. I would like to suggest an amusing image drawn from soccer games where the players form a wall to stop a free kick. Their reflex is to place their two hands crossed over their genitals to protect themselves from the ball. This is a comical image that brings to mind a row of little boys, all worried about their bodies and it is also a striking illustration of the way in which man sees his sex as being his most intimate Achilles tendon. But the most amusing part of this soccer story is to note that when the player of the other team finally takes his free kick, the defenders in the wall, still protecting their genitals, spontaneously flinch as if they fear being struck by the ball, and sometimes, against all expectation, leap in place to avoid the ball at the risk of letting it pass between their legs and roll into the net. Concerned with self-preservation, they neglect their mission, which is to block the ball. Similarly when his virility is in danger, man is just as concerned with protecting it as the soccer player was to protect his genitals. He can risk everything, even his life, but never his pride of being virile. Now who are those, who, in the life of the man, can do him harm, take his power from him, menace his virility or humiliate him, if not the father who is admired and feared as well as the woman, I mean the woman who is his rival? Who, other than the admired father and the rival woman, can steal his power? In any case, it is not the mother! On the contrary she nourishes his force, and convinces him of the exceptional destiny that awaits him...This is why I always recommend to a mother that she tell her son all the confidence she has in him and to support him in his projects, not to support him in his beauty or image, but in his power to make and create. In fact, to speak to him of his looks and charm would reinforce rather his bad narcissism, that of the image, and weaken his ego. No, it is decidedly not the mother who threatens the child but rather the idealized father and the vindictive woman. In short, his sex, his virility, and his force, are the most sacred things for a man, and must be defended at any cost.

The Fruits of the Oedipus Complex: The Super-Ego and Sexual Identity

Once resolved, I would like to say, insufficiently resolved, since the de-sexualization of the parents is never complete and the anxiety is never definitively repressed, the masculine Oedipus complex will have two decisive consequences for the formation of the future personality of the boy. On the one hand, there is the birth of a new psychical agency, the super-ego, and on the other hand, the confirmation of a sexual identity that was already initiated at around two years of age and is affirmed more concretely after puberty. The super-ego is instituted by virtue of a surprising psychical gesture: the boy abandons his parents as sexual objects and keeps them as his objects of identification. Since he can no longer have them as objects of his desire, he appropriates them as objects of his ego. The unconscious wish of *being* like them, in their ambitions, in their weakness, and in their ideals, replaces the impossibility of *having* them as sexual partners. Unable to possess them sexually, he assimilates their morality. It is due to this incorporation that the child integrates the parental prohibitions that he will henceforth impose on himself. The result of this passage from sexuality to morality is what one calls the super-ego and the feelings that express it: modesty, the sense of intimacy, shame, and moral tactfulness.

The second fruit of Oedipus is the gradual assumption of sexual identity. Before Oedipus, the child had a rudimentary and intuitive knowledge of sexual difference without yet being able to identify itself as a girl or a boy, or affirm that his father is a man or mother a woman. At the beginning of Oedipus, he does not always identify the sex of his father, of his mother or of his brothers and sisters. Note that at three years of age, there is no difference between men and women, masculine or feminine, but only between those who have the Phallus and those who do not have the Phallus, between the strong and the weak. However, the social, linguistic, and familial contexts, as well as the erogenous sensations emanating from the genital region, and the feeling of being attracted by the parent of the opposite sex, are the factors that gradually establish the basis of a sexual identity that will not truly be acquired until much later, at the age of puberty. It is then that the young adolescent will integrate the idea that the penis is an exclusive attribute of the man, and if he has already discovered the vagina, that the vagina is an exclusive attribute of the woman. Little by little, he forges a sexual identity of a man by discovering that masculinity and femininity are above all comportments that do not necessarily correspond to the physiological anatomical reality of a man or a woman. He learns that all humans, by their bisexual constitution, possess both masculine and feminine traits. He perhaps concludes from this that sexual difference will always remain an enigma for us. The reader can refer to Diagram 8 (pp. 88–89) for a chart comparing virile and feminine types. This chart is to be read as a range of dominant traits that characterize the behavior of a man and woman from the point of view of the Oedipus complex, and not as an account of normative traits.

Summary of the Logic of the Boy's Oedipus

Before discussing the girl's Oedipus complex, I would like to summarize the different phases of that the Oedipal boy goes through, by letting him speak for himself. Let us listen:

"I am four years old. I feel sensations in my penis. → I have the Phallus and I believe myself to be omnipotent. → I desire to possess my parents sexually, be possessed by them and suppress my father. → I gain pleasure from fantasizing about my incestuous desires. → My father threatens to punish me by castrating me. → I see the nude body of a little girl or of my mother and observe the absence of the penis. → I am even more afraid of being punished. → Anxious, I prefer to renounce my desire for my parents in order to save my penis. → I forget everything: desires, fantasms, and anxiety. I detach myself sexually from my parents and make their morality mine. → I begin to understand that my father is a man and that my mother is a woman, and I gradually realize that I belong to the male line. → Later, as an adolescent, my Oedipal fantasies awaken, but at that age my strict super-ego will oppose them. This battle between fantasms and the super-ego will manifest itself through the excessive and conflictual attitudes that are proper to adolescence: excessive modesty, inhibitions, fear, and contempt of women, and the rejection of established values."

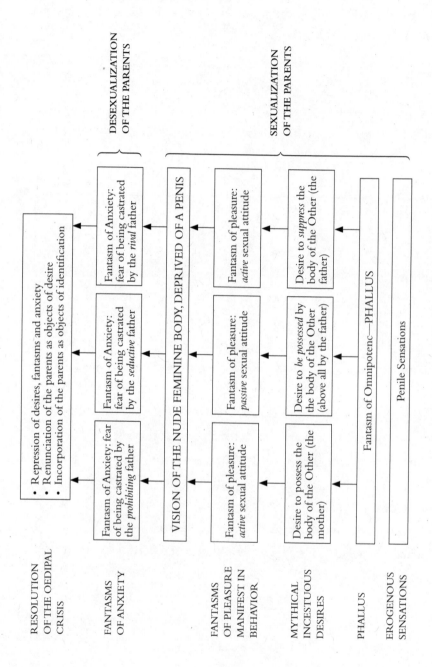

Diagram 2   Logic of the Oedipus of the Boy

The Oedipus of the Girl

A Pre-Oedipal Time: The Girl Is Like a Boy

A Time of Solitude: The Girl Feels Alone and Humiliated

The Time of Oedipus: The Girl Desires Her Father

The Resolution of Oedipus: The Woman Desires a Man

The Most Feminine Woman Always Has Her Father within Her

Summary of the Logic of the Girl's Oedipus Complex

A Pre-Oedipal Time: The Girl Is Like a Boy

(See Diagram 3, which accompanies this chapter.)

I am going to tell you the rest of our metapsychological legend now by describing the four stages of the feminine Oedipus. You will immediately recognize that we are in a world that is completely different from that of the masculine Oedipus. While three incestuous desires coexist in the four-year-old boy (the desire to possess, to be possessed, and desire to suppress the Other), with respect to a girl of the same age, there is only one incestuous desire in the beginning: that of *possessing the mother*, followed later by that of *being possessed by the father*. I indeed say, "to possess the mother," even if that seems surprising for a girl. In this respect a clarification is necessary. If you accept the current interpretation of the word *Oedipus* as the child's erotic attraction to the parent of the opposite sex, we cannot say that the little girl's desire to possess the mother is Oedipal. It is, rather, pre-Oedipal in the sense that is considered necessary to accede to the father in order to actually enter into the Oedipus Complex. It is thus by first *sexualizing* her mother that the girl will then be able to *sexualize* her father. This is why Freud called the stage preparatory to the sexualization of the father the "pre-Oedipal phase." For his part, the boy has no need for this preliminary phase since he desires the parent of the opposite sex from the outset, that is to say, his mother. And the mother will be the sole object of his Oedipal desire. We have seen that the boy always has his mother as object, even if, with respect to the fantasm of the seduction of the boy, I have demonstrated that the father can also be the object of desire for his son. However, in a classical sense one can say that the boy only desires one sexual object, his mother, while the girl desires two: first, the mother, then the father.

Now, early in the twenty-first century, I must remind you of the numerous and vigorous debates that took place between psychoanalysts in the 1930s concerning the importance of pre-Oedipal stage in the life of a woman. In fact, this stage is essential for understanding the problematic nature of the neurotic female patients that we see every day. When I listen to a woman, I always think of the relation of this analysand to her mother, and similarly, when I listen to a man, I think most often of his relation to his father. Certainly, I am presenting a theory of the Oedipus complex but I would like to share with you the effects of Oedipus in clinical experience, and above all, explain that the problem of neurosis resides in the painful return in the adult of an *inverted Oedipus*. That is to say, the return of what was, in childhood, the sexual attraction to the parent of the *same* sex. Girls become neurotic more easily from her relation to her mother, and boys neurotic more easily from his relation to his father. Therefore, one must say that the masculine neurosis results from the boy's fixation on the father, and the feminine neurosis from the girl's fixation on the mother. If, as a practitioner, you listen to a neurotic man, think above all of his father, and in the presence of a neurotic woman, think rather of her mother.

Let's leave clinical experience for the moment and consider the following expression: "to enter into Oedipus." When can we say that a little girl enters into Oedipus? Our response is different from the one we had for the boy. The boy *enters* directly into Oedipus because he desires his mother straightaway and he *leaves* Oedipus when he desires a woman other than his mother. The girl, for her part, *enters* into Oedipus—that is to say, sexualizes her father—after having passed through the pre-Oedipal stage in the course of which she sexualized and then rejected her mother, and *leaves* Oedipus when she desires a man other than her father. A second dissymmetry between the boy and the girl concerns the rapidity with which they leave Oedipus. The boy, we have seen, simultaneously desexualizes both his parents in a quick and brutal and manner, while the girl first desexualizes the mother and later, very slowly, detaches herself sexually from her father. *The boy leaves Oedipus in a day, the girl in several years*. Therefore, we could say that the boy becomes a man in one stroke while the girl becomes a woman gradually.

But let us return to the pre-Oedipal period when the girl desires her mother as a sexual object. She adopts the same attitude as the Oedipal boy toward the mother. Like her brother, she believes she has a Phallus and reveals in her comportment that she is guided by fantasms of phallic omnipotence and of pleasure in which she plays a sexually active role in relation to her mother. Just like the boy, she feels happy, strong, and proud; she is curious, at times voyeuristic, exhibitionist, and aggressive. In sum, during this period, the little girl is animated by the incestuous desire to possess her mother, exulting in having her all to herself, and adopting a clearly masculine position, which is similar to that of the boy.

A Time of Solitude: The Girl Feels Alone and Humiliated

Now, a crucial event is going to take place that will eclipse the innocent and insolent pride of a little girl who is happy to feel all-powerful. In the same way that the boy had visually discovered the absence of the penis in the feminine body with anxiety, the girl observes the difference between her sex and that of the boy. The reaction of the little girl is immediate; she is disappointed not to have the same appendage as the boy: "He's got something I don't!" Until then she relied on her vaginal and clitoral sensations that comforted her in her feeling of omnipotence. Now that she has seen the penis, she doubts the sensations and tells herself that the source of power is not in her but in the body of the other, in the sex of the boy. The impact of the view of the penis was thus stronger than the feeling of her erogenous sensations. The disconcerting image of the penis prevailed over her intimate feelings. What she saw abolished what she felt. The girl finds herself painfully dispossessed, because the specter of power is no longer embodied in her erogenous sensations, but by the visible organ of the boy. Now the Phallus is in the other, and henceforth takes the form of a penis.

This is when an immense illusion brutally collapses, triggering an acute internal tear. I call this fantasm in which the little girl suffers from the pain of having been deprived of the precious Phallus, a "Fantasm of privation," or, more precisely, a "Fantasm of the *Pain* of privation." While the boy experienced the *anxiety* of having to lose, the little girl experiences the *pain* of having lost. While the boy dreads a *castration*, the little girl laments a *privation*.

Recall that for the boy, the fantasm that led to the resolution of Oedipus is a fantasm of anxiety. Fearing the loss of the venerated Phallus that he thought he had, the boy is led to prefer his penis to his mother. For the girl, the situation is radically different. She does not fear losing since she just determined that she does not and never will have a penis.

Contrary to the boy she has nothing to lose. No, she does not fear loss, she does not suffer anxiety, she suffers pain, the pain of having been deprived. As one can see, anxiety prevails in the boy and pain prevails in the girl. But what kind of pain? Certainly the pain of having been deprived of an invaluable object that she thought she had. Above all, however, it is the pain of having been deceived. Yes, the little girl feels deceived. Someone omnipotent has lied to her by making her believe that she had the Phallus and that she would have it forever. But who is that someone if not her own mother? A mother who was all-powerful yesterday, appears today as impotent to give her a Phallus that she herself does not have and never had. Yes, her mother is as deprived as she is and only deserves contempt and reproach.

It is at this exact moment that the embittered girl turns away from her mother and, in her solitude, is enraged at having been deprived and deceived. The pain of having been deprived and that of having been deceived are only in fact one and the same pain that I call, "the pain of humiliation," that is to say, the pain of feeling the victim of an injustice and of experiencing the wounding of her self-image. Here, the privation and the wound of self-esteem [amour propre] are conflated into one feeling, that of humiliation. The experience of privation has been experienced as an irreparable offense to the "legitimate" pride of possessing the Phallus, like a humiliating blow to her narcissism. We had said that for the boy, the narcissistic object par excellence is his precious organ, the penis-Phallus, and that his choice of saving it led him to the renunciation of his parents. For the girl, on the contrary, the narcissistic object par excellence is not a part of her body, but her self-esteem, her cherished self-image. For the girl the Phallus is not the penis but self-image. Now the immediate reaction to the wound of her self-esteem is to complain about her loss to the mother, and to complain about the harm she experienced. It is only later when the girl desires her father that the time will come for reparation, of healing and reconciliation with the mother. For the moment, the little girl is alone because she has no parents to turn to: she has rejected her mother, and does not yet have recourse to the father. It is a period of dark solitude where the girl laments her wounded narcissism. In a word, if the boy leaves Oedipus to protect his narcissism, I would say that the girl enters into Oedipus, goes to the encounter with the father in order to ask him to bandage her wounded narcissism. This can be formulated in another way. For the boy, safeguarding his penis-Phallus stopped the incestuous desire for the mother; while the need for consolation awakens a new desire in the girl, that of being possessed by her father. She abandons her mother, and for consolation, seeks her father with the hope of being possessed by him. *In the case of the boy, the narcissism of the body stops Oedipus; in the case of the girl, the narcissism of the self-image of the self opens onto Oedipus.*

The Jealous Envy of Possessing the Phallus

Let us return to an earlier stage, at that moment when the little girl discovers in the boy the penis-Phallus that she does not have. She suffers, she feels diminished [*lésée*] in her self-esteem, and claims, even demands, what belongs to her: "I want this Phallus they took from me, and I'm gonna get it, even if have to take it from him!" she yells out. This demand shows well that the pain of humiliation changed into a jealous rage of wanting to have the phallus. The girl is henceforth in the grip of a feeling that psychoanalysis calls "penis envy," and that I prefer to call "Phallus envy," in order to better emphasize that the girl does not envy the penile organ but rather the symbol of power that it incarnates in the eyes of children. **The penis does not interest her and at times even disgusts her; what interests and fascinates her is the power that she grants it and which makes her envious.** But a word of caution here! *Envy* is not synonymous with *desire.* Envy is not desire. It is one thing to envy the Phallus, and quite another to desire the penis of a man. The little girl envies the Phallus, but the woman desires the penis. Envy is a puerile feeling, while the desire for the penis is a desire proper to adulthood. Also, for a little girl to desire the penis of a man, it is still necessary that she develop into a woman, that she mature, mature her Oedipus, that is to say, that first she sexualize her father, separate from him, and later become the companion who undergoes *jouissance* from the body and the sex of the man she loves. No, Phallus envy is the infantile and jealous envy of a wounded child, spiteful and nostalgic, who wants to recuperate the symbol of power of which she believes herself to have been dispossessed. Let us note that in this imaginary duel she fights on equal footing with the boy and adopts a position of a virile rivalry.

The Time of Oedipus: The Girl Desires Her Father

At this point a new character enters the scene. It is the marvelous father, grand bearer of the Phallus. It is then that the wounded and still jealous little girl turns toward him for comfort and consolation, but to demand his power and his force. She also wants to be as strong as her father and brandish the Phallus that would make her once again master of people and things. The all-powerful father of her fantasm responds to such an ambition with a definitive refusal, by saying: *"No, I will never give you the torch of my strength, since it belongs to your mother!"* Certainly, the father who speaks in this way is a caricature, it is the father fantasized by a capricious and intransigent child. No, an adult father never speaks in this way. If he should respond to such a puerile demand, he would rather reply in the following: *"No my daughter, I cannot give you the absolute power that you attribute to me for the simple reason that it does not exist. The Phallus that you demand from me is a child's dream, even if that dream is an old fantasy* [chimère] *that has certainly led humans to love each other, but often to destroy each other. No, no one has the Phallus and no one will ever have it. My only power, my daughter, my most precious power, is the supreme power of desiring to live, of striving each moment to do what I have to do, of loving what I must do and of attempting to transmit that desire to you. It is your task, then, to transform this desire into the feminine desire of loving, of giving birth."*

This irrevocable refusal of the father is received by the girl as a crushing blow that puts an end to any hope of one day conquering the mythical Phallus. She would then understand that she will never have it, and nevertheless she does not accept it. On the contrary, she throws herself now, with all the ardor of her juvenile desire, into the arms of the father, no longer to seize his power, but to be herself the source of the power. Yes, she wishes to have the Phallus, but now she wants to go even farther, and wants *to be* the thing of the father. What does this mean? This means that the little girl wants to be herself, in every way, the precious Phallus. In other words, she wants to become the favorite of the father. Because of the first refusal of the paternal "No," the jealous *envy* of having the Phallus of the father gives way to the incestuous desire of being possessed by him, of being the Phallus of the father. When the little girl was envious, she adopted a masculine position. Now that she desires, she engages in a feminine position. The masculine feeling of envy is succeeded by the feminine desire of being possessed by the father.

This is how, by sexualizing her father—the principal actor of her fantasms—that the girl actually enters into Oedipus. The fantasm of pleasure that best illustrates the Oedipal desire of being possessed by the father is the one of being his wife, a hope expressed often by the expression: "When I am older I will marry Papa!" This entry into Oedipus is also the moment when the mother, after having been set aside, returns on the scene and fascinates her daughter with her grace and femininity. In fact, the mother who has previously been so derided is now admired as a woman who is loved and who is a model of femininity. Naturally, the little girl becomes closer to her mother and identifies with her. She identifies with her, more precisely she identifies with her mother's desire to attract and to be loved by her companion. The Oedipal behavior of the little girl is fully inspired by the feminine ideal that her mother embodies. The little girl is attentive, in every way, to learning the art of seducing men. This is the age at which girls love to watch their mothers put on their makeup, even if the admiration for the mother is accompanied by a strong rivalry. Every mother then, for her daughter, is an ideal as well as a formidable rival. This is how the first movement of the identification of the girl with the desire of the mother is accomplished, that of being the woman of the man who is loved, and of giving him a child.

The Resolution of Oedipus: The Woman Desires a Man

In the same way that the father denied the Phallus to his daughter, he now refuses, just as firmly, to take her as a sexual object, to consider her as his Phallus, that is to say, to possess her incestuously. Similarly, as the first rejection—"I will not give you my power!"—led the girl to become close to her mother and identify with her, the second rejection—"I do

not want you as a woman!"—leads the girl to identify with the person of
the father. In fact, a curious but perfectly healthy phenomenon occurs in
the development of the feminine Oedipus. Since the little girl cannot be
the sexual object of the father, she then wants to be like him: "Since you
do not want me as a woman, I will be like you!" What does this mean? It
means that the girl accepts the repression of her desire to be possessed by
the father, but does not mean that she renounces him as a person. While
the Oedipal boy resigns himself to losing his mother through cowardice,
the girl, for her part, no longer has anything to lose, and bravely persists
in trying to possess her father. She wanted to have the Phallus, but she
was denied. She wanted to be the Phallus and was dismissed; now she
wants everything, she wants the father completely and she will have him!
How? By devouring him, that is, by incorporating him and by making
him live within her. This is why I would say that the desexualization
of the father is fundamentally a mourning. The little girl mourns the
loss of her sexualized father and makes him live again as desexualized
within her. Just as the mourner who, completing his or her mourning,
ends up identifying with the deceased, the girl, having renounced the
fantasm of the father, ends up identifying with the person of the real
father. She kills her fantasmatic father, but revives him as a model of
identification. In other words, the little girl ceases to desire the father
in her Oedipal fantasms and incorporates his person into the ego. This
is how she fills herself with the attitudes, gestures, desires, and even the
moral values of her real father. She is "the spitting image" of her father.
Identified with the masculine traits of the father after having identified
with the feminine traits of the mother, the little girl finally leaves the
Oedipal scene and is henceforth open to future partners in her life as
a woman. Note the two constitutive identifications of the woman: the
identification with the femininity of the mother and the identification
with the virility of the father were triggered by the two refusals of the
father: the refusal to give the Phallus to his daughter and the refusal to
take her as Phallus.

Let us express this in another way. The encounter we just considered,
opposing the Oedipal girl to her father, inspired the brief and lively
exchange that follows between our two legendary heroes. I would like

to emphasize that the father of the following scene is healthy and in love with his wife.

LITTLE GIRL: Father, give me your power!

FATHER: No! I will do nothing of the sort. I will not give you my power, I will give it to your mother!

LITTLE GIRL: But in that case I myself would like to be your power! Please, let me be your muse, the ardent source of your power. Father, I beg of you. Look at me! I am your most precious object. Possess me!

FATHER: No! This is out of the question! You are not my wife. I have refused to give you my power and I accept you even less as its source.

LITTLE GIRL: Since that is the case, since you deprive me of your power and will not let me be your muse, then I am going to appropriate you and become like you, I mean, better than you. Yes, I am going to devour you completely and resemble you to such a point that I will walk like you, adopt your look, mimic the intensity of your gaze, strive for the brilliance of your mind and the ardor of your ambition. In this way I will be as strong as you, and, you'll see, much stronger than you!

Such is the juvenile eagerness, the pugnacious will of a little girl who will never stop trying to realize her desire to be loved, and, when the time comes, to carry a child. To love and to transmit life, when all is said and done, is the highest mission that nature assigns to the woman. It is as if nature—if there is really an entity called nature—encouraged her by telling her: "Defend desire tooth and nail, protect love and ensure the transmission of life!"

Before going farther, I would like to emphasize that psychoanalytic literature on the feminine Oedipus is vast, rich, and full of questions. Nevertheless, all authors converge toward the same conclusion by declaring that femininity remains an unresolved enigma. But recognizing one's ignorance does not help. For my part, I have attempted to explore the legend of the Oedipal girl, to engage that history and to propose a clear and detailed interpretation, inspired by psychoanalytic theory and by listening to my patients. I sought to dramatize my intuition that the girl, unlike the boy, was driven by an inextinguishable thirst for love and at the crescendo of her Oedipus: "Give me! Take me and I devour you!," was only the irresistible rise of a desire imbedded in all the fibers of her femininity.

The Most Feminine Woman Always Has Her Father in Her

> My father has left his imprint in me: he has impregnated my desire, modeled the form of my nose, set the rhythm of my step, and nevertheless I feel the most feminine of women.— Statement of a patient

I would like to dwell for a moment on the identification of the girl with the person of her father. From the clinical point of view, one can hardly imagine the importance that the fantasm of the father has in the life of a woman. When you listen to a woman who suffers, ask yourself two things. First, as I mentioned above, one should question the often conflictual bond that she has forged with the parent of the same sex, that is to say, with the mother. Second, ask yourself who is the father who is within her. Yes, a woman always has her father in her. Each time that I have listened to a patient, the idea comes to me that she is inhabited by her father. Certainly, this identification does not apply for all women but when there is such identification, and when you are a good observer, one can easily discern the father in the unintentional expressions of the face of your patient, in the wrinkles of her forehead, the roughness of her hands, in the form of her nose and especially in her demeanor and gait. It often happens that a woman unconsciously adopts the same posture and the same demeanor as her father. It is incontestable that the fantasmatic father occupies a central place in the life of a woman.

I am thinking now of the most classical familial situation. Once she has identified with her father, it happens that the girl can no longer stand her true father, her flesh and blood father. She is often angry with him and criticizes his faults and weaknesses, or quite simply, for being who he is. Also, the father, I mean the true father, the father we are, has before him, in the person of his daughter, the incarnation of his own super-ego. His daughter has become for him, without her even knowing it, his most formidable rival, and he has become for her, her most intolerable mirror.

One final remark on the pathology of the identification of the girl with the father: when this introjection is not counterbalanced by the identification with the mother, one of the most tenacious feminine neuroses settles in. I call this the *hysteria of love*, and it consists in the rejection of amorous love. The woman, who is entirely inhabited by the fantasm of the father, cannot engage in a lasting intimate relationship. All of her of love sensors are saturated by the paternal omnipresence. She has no lover but remains strongly inhabited by the father she loves. She is alone and unsatisfied but filled by her secret passion. She is neither spiteful nor hateful toward men; she has simply withdrawn from an amorous and sexual life. In brief, she prefers to keep her father inside her rather than engage in an affective relation, which would always be fragile, because she feels exposed to the risk of being abandoned.

However, except for this possible neurotic predicament that is due to an overwhelming identification with the father, the little girl will allow the feminine and masculine traits borrowed from the mother and the father to express themselves within her. This is precisely the most frequent ending of the feminine Oedipus. Indeed, the end of Oedipus is, in effect, a long path in the course of which the little girl, becoming a woman, will adopt both masculine and feminist traits, and progressively change her desire of being possessed by the father into a desire of being possessed by a man she loves. One observes, in this respect, a slow desexualization of the Oedipal relation to the father, and correlatively the assumption of her feminine identity.

How is the Oedipus of the girl resolved? I am proposing what could be seen as the ideal resolution of the complex. The painful fantasm of having been deprived of an all-powerful Phallus has definitively vanished. Now the young girl in her becoming a woman has completely forgotten the puerile alternative of having or not having the Phallus. She no longer measures her being or her sex against a supposed masculine Phallus. She has mourned the illusory Phallus and has determined that her sex is

something other than the lack of a lost Phallus. She has also overcome
the infantile idea that made the woman an inferior and castrated being,
and she no longer blames her mother and no longer competes with
her for men. The young girl discovers the vagina, the desire of being
penetrated and of undergoing *jouissance* from the penis in a sexual union.
She also discovers the uterus and her desire to carry the child of the
man she loves.

One more word before concluding, in order to dispel a frequent
misunderstanding: some have believed that psychoanalysis, founded on
the concept of the Phallus, conceives of the woman as castrated and
inferior. That is absurd! The only thing psychoanalysis has done—and
that was a genuine revolution—was to discover that human beings are
inhabited by fantasms as morbid as the most toxic virus, and the most
virulent of these fantasms is that of representing the woman as a castrated
and inferior being. This fantasm is above all an infantile illusion. I know
that this puerile representation is just as present in the minds of numerous
neurotic adults. It is precisely the neurotics who believe that the woman
is a castrated being. However, quite obviously, this is false. The sex of
a woman is in no way the lack of anything! The woman has her own
sex and she is proud of it. Whether it is a question of her vagina, her
breasts, her skin, or the entire erogenous body, the woman is happy to
be what she is. But how can the neurotic, whether man or woman, take
the woman to be inferior? Because the neurotic is talking about him or
herself. He or she is the weak woman! Fixated on his or her infantile
fantasm, the neurotic lives with the fear of being castrated. Thus, all his
or her affective relations are experienced in a defensive mode. He or she
is always on the defensive in order to parry any abuse or any humiliation from those around him or her, from those on whom the neurotic
depends…and on whom he or she would never wish to depend. It is as
if, in his fantasms, the neurotic says, "They will not have me! I am not a
little girl [*femmelette*]!" or as if the neurotic woman says, "I am not their
servant!" Certainly, psychoanalysis postulates that the Phallus exists and
that the woman is castrated, but, as has been noted, the Phallus is an
illusion and the woman is only castrated in the unconscious imagination
of children and of neurotics.

Summary of the Logic of the Girl's Oedipus Complex

As in the case of the Oedipal experience of the boy, let us consider now the testimony of the girl:

PreOedipal Stage	I am four years old. I feel clitoral excitations → I have the phallus, I am proud of it and I feel omnipotent → **Just like a boy I desire to possess my mother →**	The girl is a boy
Stage of Solitude	Faced with a completely nude little boy, **I discover that I do not have The Phallus →** I suffer from being deprived of it → I realize that my mother is also deprived → I blame her for having made me believe that we both had it → She therefore deceived me → Vexed, I leave my mother → Now I feel alone and humiliated. My self-esteem is wounded → I am jealous of the boy →	The girl feels alone and humiliated
Oedipal Stage	I turn now toward my father, the great keeper of the Phallus → Still jealous and envious I ask him to give it to me → **He refuses to give it to me →** I understand that I will never have it → I ask my father to console me → My envy has become desire. I no longer want to have my father's Phallus, I want to be it; I want to be my father's favorite → Then, I identify with my mother as a desired woman and model of femininity → **I desire to be possessed by my father →**	The girl desires her father
The Resolution of Oedipus	**My father refuses →** I desexualize my father, **but incorporate his person →** Gradually, I become a woman and open myself to a man I love → I no longer measure my sex against the mythical Phallus and discover the Vagina, the uterus, and the desire to bear a child for my companion.	The woman desires a man

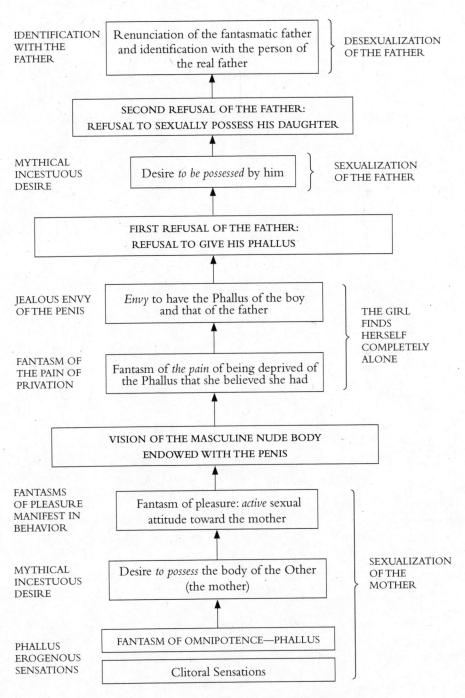

Diagram 3   Logic of the Oedipus of the Girl

Questions and
Answers Concerning Oedipus

For what problem is the concept of Oedipus a solution?

You often say that a psychoanalytic concept is a response to a question. What would be the question that led to Oedipus?*

Good question! A psychoanalytic concept is only worthwhile if it shows itself to be indispensable to the coherence of the theory and useful to our practice. This is a principle that is even more true when it concerns a notion that is as important as the one I just discussed. For what problem, then, is Oedipus a solution? For me, Oedipus is the response to two questions: First, what gives form to the sexual identity of a man and a woman, and second, how does a person become neurotic? The problem for which Oedipus is the solution is that of the origin of our adult sexuality, and further, of the origin of our numerous neurotic sufferings. These two questions—sexuality and neurosis—are so intricately entwined that one can say that the neurosis results from a disturbed infantile sexuality, arrested in its maturation, hypertrophic, or on the contrary, inhibited. At bottom, Oedipus enables us to understand how an erotic pleasure that affects a four-year-old child can be transformed into a neurotic pain that afflicts the forty-year-old person he or she has become.

I would like to formulate the same idea, but by recalling what led Freud to the discovery of the Oedipus Complex. From what source did

---

*The questions in this section were gathered from various members of the audience who attended a number of lectures that have I delivered concerning Oedipus.

Freud derive the idea of Oedipus? From the observation of children? Absolutely not. Of course he was attentive to their behavior, but he did not conceive of the idea of Oedipus by studying the parent-child relation, even if the familial reality, whether that of yesterday or today, confirms the Freudian discovery on a daily basis. No, it was not children who introduced Oedipus. We should suppose, then, that Freud's invention stemmed from Freud's self-analysis. Actually, it was through his dreams, through the analysis of his dreams, by evoking his childhood and addressing his written reflections to his friend and correspondent Wilhelm Fliess that Freud elaborated Oedipus. It was an Oedipus essentially dominated by the desire of parricide and the resulting guilt, especially since the idea of Oedipus was revealed for the first time in 1897, when his father Jacob Freud died. However, it was not from his own introspection that Freud grasped what was essential with respect to this nodal concept of psychoanalysis. My hypothesis is quite different. For me, Oedipus is an invention forged by Freud as a result of listening to his adult patients. Let me now tell you a fictitious story.

We are in Vienna in 1896, in the consultation office at 19 Bergstrasse, at the moment when Freud received a hysterical patient who spoke to him of her childhood. While listening attentively, Freud sought to confirm the thesis he had recently developed concerning the etiology of hysteria. Indeed, at that time, he thought that hysteria was provoked by the incapacity of the patient to recall a sexual trauma that occurred in the first years of his or her life. As a child, he told himself, the female patient would have suffered sexual abuse committed by an adult. It would be the persistent oblivion of this scene of seduction that would have made her neurotic. While the scene of seduction remains repressed in the unconscious, it is manifested in painful symptoms; but it suffices to make it conscious so as to diminish its virulence. Precisely in order to cure hysteria, Freud said, it is necessary for the scenes with latent sexual content buried in the unconscious to become conscious, which is the sole condition for them to weaken and cease being pathogenic. Thus, Freud listened to his young hysteric by trying to discern if in her childhood she had been seduced by an adult and, if so, then by trying to make her narrate the details of the incident to him, and above all, to help her relive her traumatic experience. Many among us know that, years later, Freud made a major change in his theory. He had to recognize that these famous scenes of seduction had not necessarily taken place but that they were rather fantasms imagined by his patients. Thus, the neurotic symptoms were not the consequence of a sexual abuse that really happened, but of a sexual abuse that was fantasized and forgotten. In the end, he said, it mattered little whether it was a real event or a fantasm. The scene of an infantile sexual seduction committed by a perverse adult, remained the real cause of hysteria on the condition that it was repressed. Recall that hysteria is above all a sickness of forgetfulness, that the hysteric is hysterical because he or she does not want to remember what was painful.

But one will ask, what is the relation with Oedipus? I believe Freud discovered Oedipus by reflecting on the plot and on the actors in the scene of seduction. In the case of neurosis, the little girl is seduced by a perverse man. In the case of Oedipus, the little girl is seduced by her own father. The fantasmatic scene of seduction as a source of hysteria became, in Freud's thought, a fantasmatic scene in which the child was seduced by the father without being the victim of sexual abuse and without being affected by a toxic pleasure. It suffices for a parent to be more affectionate than usual for a child to feel that excess of tenderness as an erogenous trigger and a sexual pleasure that is too intense. But identifying the role of the father was still not the full discovery of Oedipus. It lacks the main element. I would like to be very clear here. While listening to his patient narrate a sexual incident from childhood, Freud imagined the scene, identified with the persona of the character of seduced child, and perceived that while the child was not entirely passive, he or she was also inhabited by the *active* desire of being seduced by the father. Yes, the key to Oedipus lies in the incestuous *desire of the child* to be possessed by the father. Freud discovered Oedipus by moving from a scene of seduction in which a frightened girl is a passive victim of an adult aggressor, to the Oedipal scene where an innocent and sensual girl is the unconscious instigator who incites the father or the older brother to desire her sexually. The child of the scene of seduction is a victim while the child of the Oedipal scene is a child torn between her desire to be seduced and her fear of being so, between her thirst for pleasure and her fear of experiencing it.

Now that we know the context of the discovery of Oedipus we can return to our initial question: for what problem is Oedipus the solution? Oedipus is a *fantasm of seduction* that is at the foundation of the sexual identity of any man and any woman: a fantasm of pleasure and of anxiety. Usually, this fantasm is metabolized by the child, but it can be the case that the pleasure, the anxiety, and the pain are traumatic and repressed only with difficulty. That is to say, that the emotions experienced by the Oedipal child in the situation of seduction are so violent that they remain active and foment a neurosis in the adult. The Oedipal fantasm that has not been liquidated remains virulent, comes to the surface of consciousness, and repetitively and compulsively externalizes itself in the life of the neurotic.

At what age does a child feel, for the first time, a sexual pleasure?

First, something self-evident: the sexual pleasure experienced by a child is by nature different from that experienced by an adult. That being said, we know that in interuterine life, a fetus can already have erections, which allow us to assume, if not a sexual experience, at least a genital sensation. This shows that there is no age specific to experience a sexual pleasure, as long as the body of the child is in contact with an adult who is him- or herself excited, desiring and taking pleasure from the body of the child, even if in the most tender and chaste manner. In this respect, I have some astonishing lines from Freud that I would like to mention. Freud did not hesitate "to identify tender feelings with sexual love." He affirmed that "A child's interaction with anyone responsible for his care affords him an unending source of sexual excitation and satisfaction from his erotogenic zones. This is especially so since the person in charge of him, who, after all, is as a rule his mother, herself regards him with feelings that are derived from *her own sexual life*: she strokes him, kisses him, rocks him and quite clearly treats him as a substitute for a complete sexual object. A mother would probably be horrified if she were made aware that *all her gestures of affection* were rousing the child's sexual instinct and preparing for its later intensity. She regards what she does as *asexual*, "pure" love, since, after all, she carefully avoids any unnecessary contact with the child's genitals. As we know, however, the sexual instinct is not aroused only by direct excitation of the genital zone. What we call affection will unfailingly show its effects one day on the genital zones as well" (Freud, SE, VII p. 223).

While discussing Oedipus with you I have said that sexuality was at the heart of familial love and hate, but in the preceding passage, Freud goes much further, because he does not say that the sexual lies in tenderness but that tenderness is itself a sexual excitation.

If it is true that a baby can experience sexual pleasure
in the arms of its mother, can one conclude that Oedipus
appears well before the ages of three or four?

That is precisely the position of Melanie Klein who postulates a precocious Oedipus proper to the newborn. It is also Lacan's position, who considered that there is no age proper to Oedipus since the desire of the child is only the extension of the desire of the mother. This was, in fact, Freud's position in the preceding passage. That being the case, there is a significant difference between the Kleinian Oedipus and the Freudian Oedipus. For Melanie Klein the erotic drives of a baby pertain to the mother perceived not as a whole person but as a partial object: the mother is reduced to being the breast. The Kleinian Oedipus can be an oral or an anal Oedipus. For Freud it is different. Oedipus only exists if the erotic drives of the child pertain to the mother or the father as whole persons equipped with a body, inhabited by a desire and capable of experiencing pleasure. If, for Melanie Klein, Oedipus is oral or anal, for Freud it is after the pregenital and prior to the genital, and is above all *phallic*.

How does Oedipus take place when
the mother lives alone with her child?

It can be fully verified as long as the mother desires. It does not matter if the mother lives alone. What matters is that she is attached to someone , that she desires someone; and in the case that she does not have a partner what matters is that she be interested in someone else than her child, that her love for her child is not the only love in her life. In sum, there is Oedipus when the mother desires a third between her and her child. This is the father. The father is the third that the mother desires.

> [Freud] . . . has not given a scientific explanation of the ancient myth. What he has done is to propound a new myth.
>
> —Wittgenstein*

Certainly, Freud has proposed a new myth, but what a myth! And how rich! It is thanks to this formidable theoretical apparatus that psychoanalysts today are able to listen to their patients and alleviate their suffering.

*Finally, is Oedipus a reality that can be observed
or a fantasm deduced by psychoanalysts?*

I have already shown that Oedipus was reality and fantasm at the same time, but this question is an opportunity for me to address the problem differently. One can say that the Oedipus complex is a collection of contradictory feelings of an unconscious nature reflecting the conscious feelings experienced by the child in the triangular relation with its parents. In the end, Oedipus is an *intersubjective complex engendered by an intersubjective reality*. It is very important to conceive of Oedipus as an unconscious fantasm proper to *a singular* individual even if the presence of another desiring individual is necessary—as we just saw while reading Freud—for this fantasm to form and subsist. However, one should know that the Oedipal fantasm is a hypothesis, a construction of the mind built from the behavior of children in relation to their parents, and especially from childhood memories reported by our adult patients in psychoanalysis. In fact, Oedipus is not always an observable phenomenon or a verifiable hypothesis. Psychoanalysis is not a behavioral science. No:

---

*Ludwig Wittgenstein, *Lectures & Conversations on Aesthetics, Psychology and Religious Belief*, ed. Cyril Barrett (Berkeley: University of California Press, 2007), 51.

it is necessary to take Oedipus as an efficacious theoretical schema with an undeniable impact in the affective life of an individual and in our culture. It is thus, properly speaking, a *fantasm* and a *myth*. One can say it even better: from a clinical point of view, Oedipus is a fantasm that comes from the innermost depths [*le tréfonds*] of being, and thoroughly permeates it. And from a cultural point of view, Oedipus is a myth, a myth for all of us, since it is the symbolic fable, simple and striking, which stages familial characters who incarnate the force of human desire and the prohibitions that oppose it. Now, whether a fantasm or a myth, the Oedipus complex is also an absolutely *crucial concept* that is absolutely indispensable to the coherence of the theory and the efficacy of psychoanalytic practice. I do not hesitate to tell you that without the concept of Oedipus, most of the psychoanalytic notions would be adrift, and without the fantasm of Oedipus, we could not clarify the infinite complexity of psychical suffering. Assuredly, it is thanks to this formidable conceptual apparatus that today psychoanalysts are able to listen to their patients, understand them, and alleviate their suffering. I am thinking here of a text in which Lacan already emphasized the irreplaceable theoretical value of Oedipus. Here is what he wrote in his *Proposition du Octobre 1967 sur le psychanalyste de l'École*: "I would like to clarify what illuminates my approach, simply, which is to say that, to deny Oedipus and psychoanalysis. . . , would lead to a delirium . . . ." Incontestably, Oedipus is the cornerstone of the psychoanalytic edifice: it is a *crisis* manifest in infantile sexuality; an unconscious *fantasm*; a social *myth*; and the most crucial *concept* of psychoanalysis.

In the tragedy of Sophocles the main character is destiny,
over which the heroes have no control. What is the place
of destiny of the Oedipus complex?

Let us not forget that Freud was always obsessed with destiny, by what life holds for us and that we ignore. In the end, the young Oedipus killed his father, while, paradoxically, Laïos made every attempt to escape the oracle that predicted the parricidic act of his son. No one knows nor escapes his or her destiny! Thus, no child escapes the trial of the

Oedipus complex, and it marks him or her permanently. But what is the initiatory experience that is in question? What is the unavoidable rite that we call Oedipus? It is the experience of a loss and of a mourning of the parents rendered fantasmatic as sexual partners. Yes, Oedipus is, in the life of the child, the first deep and internal detachment from the parents. It is a necessary separation that announces the future emancipation of the young adult. Whether it is a question of the feminine or masculine Oedipus, in both cases, one loses the parents ineluctably. Certainly, the child was separated from its mother at birth, spread its wings by walking, and opened its familial cocoon by going to nursery, but it is only at the end of Oedipus that the little boy or girl comes to perceive the parents differently and love them in a different way. They cease desiring them in order to learn to love them tenderly or to hate them. Of course, this is an ideal detachment since in our everyday life we always continue to desire our parents sexually, most often in the sublimated form of tenderness, and at other times, unfortunately, in the form of a painful conflict that is due to the persistence of a virulent desire.

With respect to the boy, could you address the expression:
"Inverted Oedipus"?

The inverted Oedipus is the child's sexual attraction for the parent of the same sex. Concerning the masculine Oedipus, one usually emphasizes the erotic attachment of the boy to his mother and the hateful rivalry with the father. Now it happens frequently that the masculine Oedipus centers not on the desiring relation of the son with his mother but on the desiring relation with *his father considered as a sexual partner.* Yes, the father can be, in the son's mind, a sexual partner! And this is what we call an "Inverted Oedipus." To clarify this I would discuss the Oedipus of the boy as a drama with three acts. Indeed, it is pleasing to bring the Oedipus complex to life, determined as we are by Greek tragedy. Such a rhetorical device will not only allow me to remind you of what is essential to the Oedipal dynamic in a different manner, but also to explore my idea that the principal character in the masculine Oedipus is the father more often than the mother.

Let us address the three acts of the drama, beginning with the *first act*, which includes the boy and the girl indifferently. The curtain opens and all the characters appear straightaway on the stage: a little boy, a little girl, a mother, a father, and even all the humans who inhabit our planet. Imagine a scene including a lot of people [*pleine de monde*], a world [*monde*] where everyone, in the eyes of the two children, possesses a power represented by a visible corporeal sign: the penis. In the mind of the boy or girl, everyone has a penis, or better, everyone is invested by power represented by the penis. Freud called this Oedipal moment, "*the premise of the universal possession of the phallus.*" This is the moment when the magical belief in a universe entirely populated by those who bear a marvelous penis prevails in the child. Let me reformulate this immediately and, in the place of the expression "marvelous penis," instead use "Phallus."

*Unfortunately, I have not always understood how one
passes from the penis to the Phallus. Precisely, what
do you understand by the Phallus?*

Phallus is the name we give to the fantasm of the penis, to the subjective interpretation of the penis, to the way that each of us perceives the penile appendage. More generally we use the word *Phallus* to designate the fantasm of any object that bears, as seen through our child's eyes—even when we are adults—the highest affective value. When I say "through our child's eyes," it is to explain that the passionate love that we give to a person or to an object is always a child's love, since love is only a refinement of childhood candor. To love is to believe in all innocence—and this innocence is precious to us—that the other, our loved one, will someday complete us. This superb hope of love makes me happy, reassures me, and gives me strength. Similarly, any object that is loved, admired, and possessed reassures and comforts me in my feeling of being myself. Now, this object that is so invested and charged with all my affectivity, and which is indispensable for me, is called the Phallus. This is why the word *Phallus* designates not only the penis as fantasm, that is to say, when it is experienced as the symbol of the power, but also any person, object, or ideal to which I am viscerally attached, on which

I am dependent, and that I feel is the source of my power. Phallus is thus the name that we give to anything highly invested; so invested and so loved, that it ceases to be concrete and becomes a fantasm. A mother, a father, our partner, the penis, the clitoris, or even a house, a career, a promotion, are all concrete supports that can become our Phallus. Now, what concrete thing gives the Oedipal child the feeling of having a Phallus? I propose that it is the body, his or her own body, the body of sensations. Indeed, for the little boy, the real seat of the Phallus is his own little sex as an erogenous appendage, or the excitations emanating from the testicles or the groin. For the girl, the real seat of the Phallus is the collection of erogenous sensations emanating from her genital organs, and in particular, from her clitoris.

If I understand you, a mother can be, for example, in the eyes
of her son, a bearer of the Phallus as well as the Phallus itself?

Absolutely. When the mother imposes her authority, she *has* the Phallus; but when the child feels she is entirely his or hers, she *is* his or her Phallus. If my mother is angry with me she is phallic and all-powerful. If, on the other hand, I argue with my friend about who has the prettiest mother, my mother is my most precious Phallus. You see that a mother can be fantasized in a twofold way, both as *having* the Phallus and as *being* the Phallus.

A boy can then have two forms of the Phallus:
his penis and his mother?

Of course, and this will be the very problem that the Oedipal boy will have to resolve; unable to keep both forms of the Phallus, he will have to choose one of them: his penis or his mother. But let us not anticipate since this crucial choice will only be made in the second act of our Oedipal drama. For the moment, let's remain in the first act. I stated earlier that the child believes that all humans are endowed with the same attribute that he or she holds so dearly: the Phallus. Boy or girl, the child feels erogenous sensations, observes his or her sex, touches him or herself, feels all-powerful, and silently looks at the characters around him or her, attributing to them a similar feeling of omnipotence. It is indeed in the perception of oneself and of the other that the magical belief in a universal Phallus is forged in silence. To see, to feel and to believe are thus the three first mute gestures of the Oedipal child. Basically, boys and girls inaugurate their Oedipus on the basis of the illusion that elevates the Phallus or its corporeal representative, the penis, to the level of a universal attribute. This is the first act of our drama in which everyone is strong. This is an essential act but is often forgotten in psychoanalytic literature, even though it is the obligatory step for access to the concept of castration anxiety. Why? Because it would be first necessary to have believed that one is strong and rich for the fear of being dispossessed to appear.

Now we can address the *second act* of the masculine Oedipus. The Oedipus of the girl follows a different scenario. Now we can justify our proposition according to which *it is the father and not the mother who is the principal character in the Oedipus of the boy*. Here is the argument. Always inhabited by the illusion of a universal Phallus, the boy forges two essential affective relations: one relation of *desire* with his mother considered as a sexual object, and above all relation of *love* with his father taken as a model to be imitated. The little boy makes his father an ideal that he would like to resemble. In a word the bond with the mother—as sexual object—is nothing other for the boy than the appetite of a desire, while his bond with the father—as ideal object—rests on a feeling of love. These two motions—desire for the mother and love for the father—relate to each other, finally encounter each other, and it is from this encounter of sensations that the Oedipus complex results. I translate this by saying that for the boy the normal Oedipus complex means to desire his mother and resemble his father.

Let us enter now into the *third act*. Suddenly, the little boy is troubled by the imposing presence of a rival who prevents him from reaching his mother. The child then feels threatened by a competitor who is stronger than he. Under the effect of the anxiety of being harmed—castration anxiety—the little boy will finally renounce the desire to possess the mother and eliminate the father. Now the dramatic turn of events. Here

an unintended reversal of the situation takes place. Threatened by castration and lacking an object on which to attach his choice, the boy returns
suddenly to his father and asks himself, "Why not change partner? Why
not him? In the place of satisfying my desire to possess a woman, I could
be satisfied equally by letting myself be possessed by a man who is strong
and virile." What has happened? Everything is upside down. From the
ideal that evoked admiration and from a rival who inspired fear, the father
has become, for the boy, a person who excites his desire. Before, the father
was the one he wanted *to be*, an ideal. Now the father is the one that
the boy would like *to have* by offering himself to him. In effect it often
happens that the little boy reacts to the threat of castration from an overly
severe father by putting himself in the place of a submissive woman, an
object of paternal desire. This is how I conceive of the *inverted Oedipus*, an
expression that is used often and rarely understood. The inverted Oedipus,
which is so important for our understanding of the origin of masculine
neurosis, consists in a radical reversal of the feelings of the little boy in
relation to his father: the father—as an object of admiration, hate, and
dread—appears now in the eyes of the child as a possible sexual partner
to whom he would like to give himself. The desire to possess the mother
is reversed into a desire to be possessed by the father, and the desire to
eliminate [*d'écarter*] the father has been transformed into a desire to attract
him. This is the double inversion of the classical configuration of the
masculine Oedipus. Thus, the father appears in the eyes of the little boy as
four different figures: *loved* as an ideal, *hated* and *feared* as a rival, and *desired*
as a sexual partner to whom he gives himself. Of these four movements:
love, hate, fear, and desire for the father, it is above all desire that I want
to emphasize because of its importance in the formation of the sexual
identity of the future young man. But please note that it is not because
the boy loves his father that he will necessarily become homosexual or
neurotic. Certainly, when he is an adult he will be marked by a strange
tenderness and delicate sensibility, without necessarily suffering from
neurotic difficulties. Briefly, my position is essentially that the masculine neurosis is most often provoked by an inverted Oedipus that has
congealed in an invasive fantasm. The problem of the neurotic is always
a conflictual relation with the parent of the same sex.

A final corollary to the Oedipus of the boy: the distinctive feature of the father—loved as an ideal, hated and feared as a rival, and desired as a sexual object—will define the normal super-ego of the young boy. In effect, the super-ego is the result of the incorporation of these four faces of the father into the ego. It is due to this interjection that the child finally begins to separate himself from his actual father because he feels differently about him. Something has changed in the internal disposition of the boy in relation to the father. He separates himself from the real father but keeps him in his ego as a super-ego that urges him to attain an ideal, a super-ego that is at times cruel and feared in order to punish a mistake, at times arousing in order to provoke a desire, but always fostering the feeling of modesty that is necessary for a social life.

But where, in this drama that you have set forth,
do you situate the castration complex?

The castration complex is situated precisely in the third act. Castration always means anxiety because there is only castration in the form of an anxiety producing threat that weighs on the subject. If we set aside the case of the inverted Oedipus and remain within the context of the classical Oedipus according to which the boy incestuously desires his mother, we can identify three causes that provoke castration anxiety. First, quite simply, the actual presence of the person of the father. We have seen that this is a presence that produces anxiety. Then, the imperious voice of the father that commands the son: "You must not . . . You do not have the right to persist in your desire! Otherwise you will have to deal with me!" Let us note that this threat can come from a mother or from an aunt, just as well, but it invariably expresses a social law with paternal authority. The person who announces the prohibition is not important. What matters is the paternal character of an incontestable law. Let me be clear: it is because the law is incontestable that it is paternal. In effect, the law of the prohibition of incest and all the laws in general carry the seal of paternal authority because they are not negotiable. It does not matter that the voice that announces the prohibition is masculine or feminine. What matters is the firmness of the tone with which it is said.

It is necessary that the threat be uttered by a firm and calm authority that can judge, condemn, and punish: "You must not sleep with your mother or treat her as a sexual object, or you will be punished!" Punished how? "Punished by the castration of your penis, or better, punished by the castration of that which animates your arrogant omnipotence." Finally, the third cause of anxiety no longer consists in the verbal threat through the voice a censor but in a threat suggested during a visual experience. The boy—for we are still in the masculine Oedipus—discovers one day, in the nude body of his mother or of a little girl, the obscure shadow of an absence. While observing the lack of a penis in the pubic area, he is afraid and becomes anxious: "If she does not have a penis," he tells himself, "then she does not have power. If a person exists without a penis, that means that I also risk being deprived of it."

In short, crushed by the imposing presence of the person of the father, threatened by the punitive law and struck by the visual discovery that there are persons who are castrated, the anguished little boy represses his incestuous desires and fantasms and moderates his pleasure. Often—this is the thesis of the inverted Oedipus—the anxiety-ridden boy takes cowardly refuge in a position of feminine submission in relation to his father. This is when he experiences a new castration anxiety awoken by the risk of losing his *virility*. While in the masculine Oedipus where the mother is the incestuous object, the threat of castration concerns the Phallus-penis, in the inverted Oedipus where the father is the incestuous object, the castration threat concerns Phallus-virility.

It is therefore anxiety that causes the child
to recoil and separate from the parents?

Yes, absolutely. Let us consider the case of the mother. The boy is afraid and detaches himself from his mother. This is why I would say that his anxiety is a healthy one because, thanks to it, the child is forced to separate itself from the person who is the closest, from whom it necessarily had to—following the order of human affairs—distance itself. For the first time in the history of the evolution of its libido, the child finds itself facing the decisive moment of a choice: "Either you cease desiring your mother or you lose your power!" This is a crucial choice: "Either I choose the incestuous object or I preserve myself narcissistically. Either I keep my mother or I keep my penis. Of course, it is my penis that I will keep!" Let us note that this kind of dramatic alternative evokes the important choices that we often face in our adult life. As soon as we want to accomplish our desire, we observe the appearance of anxiety. "Am I capable of this? Am I not going to lose everything?" At the moment of deciding and acting, anxiety surges forth. Now, according to the Oedipal experience such as I interpret it, we always choose the narcissistic object, that is to say, we always choose to preserve ourselves, ourselves and our body. The human being is decidedly fearful and narcissistic: faced with danger, it often relinquishes the object of its desire while seeking to save its skin. Here I hear a hypothetical super-ego that would reassure the trembling man before the risks inherent in the affirmation of his desire. It would tell him: "Do not be afraid! Let yourself be carried by your desire. Follow your path. Go where your destiny awaits you!"

But another remarkable phenomenon happens. Another loss will take place, a loss much more important than that of the mother. Certainly, the boy loses his mother and preserves the penis, but he soon discovers that without the object of desire, that is to say, without the mother, the penis ultimately loses its Phallic value. "What is the point of feeling powerful if there is not an other who desires me?" Certainly, the penis is useful, but on the condition that there is a desiring and desirable other. The boy loses his mother and simultaneously loses the phallic value of his penis. Ultimately, this loss of value is a thousand times more important than the loss of the mother, which is already, without question, a fundamental experience. Better still, the Oedipal drama is the most beautiful lesson that teaches us how the things we have struggled mightily for, are, in the end, of relative value. The Oedipus myth has an extraordinary ethical scope. One can always say: "But Oedipus . . . the castration complex . . . things have evolved since a hundred years ago . . . culture, sexuality, are no longer the same . . . one can very well do without the Oedipus complex . . . etc." I would be willing to do without the Oedipus myth, but then one would have to reinvent a new one that would account for the profound meaning of the life experiences that we adults continually endure. The first experience is that of accepting the fact that faced with a difficult choice, I would never lose everything, and that if I win I would never win without some loss.

We have just seen how the scene plays out for the boy.
What is the case for the girl?

The scenario of the feminine Oedipus is very different. Let us recall that during the first act of the Oedipal drama, there is, as for the boy, the premise of the universal possession of the Phallus: everyone bears the phallus and consequently, everyone is strong! However, for the girl, and unlike the boy, there is a prehistory of Oedipus and a kind of "post-history" that are absent from the masculine Oedipus. The prehistory of the feminine Oedipus complex is knotted in the extremely tight bond between the mother and the daughter. Even prior to the onset of the phallic phase at the moment nursing at the breast the mother appears to her daughter as an object of desire, but above all as an object that nourishes her narcissism and adds to her power. In a word, the mother assumes the place of the Phallus for the little girl. At the dawn of the feminine Oedipus, the object of desire for the little girl, as for the boy, is first the breast, and immediately after weaning, the person of the mother. The dominant erogenous zone is the mouth. During the oral stage the maternal breast represents the most tender phallus. We can add another essential element of the feminine Oedipus. Upon weaning, the little girl experiences a bitter feeling toward the mother who just deprived her of the pleasure of nursing. The loss of the breast evokes a hostility in the baby girl that will be reactivated later during the phallic phase itself. Let us note that this bitterness provoked by weaning is, according to Freud, more tempered in the boy. Later the Phallus of the girl is no longer represented by the mother as an incestuous object, but by the force attributed to the father. The feminine Oedipus culminates at the moment when the girl, having already experienced the separation from her mother, is thus prepared to desire her father, to renounce him, to introject the features of his person and his values, and finally to replace him, once a young girl, by a masculine partner.

Why affirm that the girl hates her mother during
the weaning? What can be said of the castration complex
with respect to the woman?

There are many misunderstandings concerning the castration complex in women. One wrongly believes that there is no castration in the woman since her body is deprived of the penis and that she has no organ to be castrated. That is not the case. According to Freud, the castration complex in the woman does exist, but I prefer, after having established the logic of the feminine Oedipus, to refer to it as the *privation complex*. This complex begins with a visual impression: the girl sees the nude body of a boy and concludes by comparison that not only is she deprived of the penis but that she is deprived of the power that the penis signifies, that is to say, the Phallus. The absence of the penis leads her to lose the illusion of the universal premise of the phallus and to feel the envy of having it. Of having what? Not the penis in itself but the allusion of power to which the organ gives rise. This thirst for power, I call phallus envy and not penis envy. I believe profoundly in the clinical interest in presenting the concept of the feminine envy of the phallus in this way, because in the treatment of hysterical women it is always the problem of power and the neurotic fear of being dominated that prevail. With the awareness of being dispossessed, a series of feelings surge in the little girl: first, a disillusion and then the nostalgia for this illusory power, and then, above all, a rancor toward the mother who did not—the classical sentence would be—"who did not give it to her . . ." But I prefer to speak of a rancor toward the mother who was unable to prepare her for this discovery, to spare her the moment when she was going to discover the loss of her illusion. It is as if she said, "Mommy you knew already that I was going to be disappointed. Why didn't you warn me?" It is thus a rancor toward the mother, a rancor that actualizes the old hate provoked by the weaning of the first pre-Oedipal period.

Is it then not anxiety which is prevalent in the little girl?

No! In these moments one observes no anxiety. If the principal feelings of the masculine Oedipus are desire and anxiety, those of the feminine

Oedipus are above all desire, pain, and envy. Nonetheless, we recognize an anxiety typical of the adult woman. It is a particular anxiety that Freud addressed only at the end of his work. The feminine anxiety is often forgotten in psychoanalytic work since one is overly inclined to think that anxiety remains the distinctive trait of the boy while the girl would be affected by envy or hate. In the clinic, we often observe an anxiety proper to the woman. It is the anxiety of losing the love she received from the loved one. In the woman, the fear is not so much finding love as losing the love that she has. For the woman the Phallus is love itself, the inestimable thing that can never be lost!

Oedipus Is the Cause
of Ordinary and Morbid Neuroses
for Men and Women

An Ordinary Neurosis Results from the Insufficient Repression of
the Oedipus Complex; A Morbid Neurosis Results from a Traumatic
Experience of the Oedipus Complex

For this reason infantile sexuality, which is held under repression, acts as the chief motive force in the formation of symptoms; and the essential part of its content, the Oedipus Complex, is the nuclear complex of neuroses.

> —Freud, "A Child is Being Beaten"

What, finally, is a neurosis? A neurosis is a psychical suffering that is provoked by the coexistence of contradictory feelings, of love, hate, fear, and incestuous desires toward those that one loves and on whom one depends. Given this definition, we would say that Oedipus is not only, as we will see, the origin of adult neuroses, but that it is itself a neurosis, the first healthy neurosis in the life of the individual; the second is that of the crisis of adolescence. But in what way is Oedipus a neurosis? The issue concerns the gap between a child's ego as it is being formed and a torrent of overflowing drives. The ego of the child does not yet have the means of holding back the impetuous rise of its desires. This effort of the ego to contain and assimilate the panic of desire is manifest in the little child as feelings, statements, and contradictory behavior toward its parents. The child's ambivalent, indeed incoherent attitude, will be firmly established in the personality of the subject as a model for all attitudes he or she will adopt as an adult toward all those who will awaken the desire of possessing, being possessed by, and of destroying the other. This is why one can say that our everyday and always unavoidable conflicts with those around us are but natural extensions, almost as a reflex, of our infantile neurosis known as Oedipus. In other words, our everyday conflicts come from the fact that within our most noble and chaste feelings toward those we love, our incestuous sexual desires simmer. The tension of any current neurosis is thus provoked by our impossibility to fully realize, or, on the contrary, to totally avoid our incestuous drives. Thus, we shall say that Oedipus, the first healthy neurosis in life, is the origin of our ordinary painful adult neurosis, a neurosis certainly painful but, when all is said and done, tolerable and, perhaps a buffer against the madness of drives that always threaten to explode within each of us.

That being the case, it can frequently happen during the Oedipal period that the child is overcome by sensations of pleasure or pain that are too intense, and that these sensations mark the child forever as indelible traumas. Also, these childhood traumas will be the cause not of an ordinary neurosis but of a morbid neurosis that establishes itself in adolescence and persists until adulthood. There are two main variations of the neurotic return of Oedipus with adulthood: the ordinary neurosis and morbid neurosis. Ordinary *neurosis* is a conflict with those whom we intimately love because we always continue to desire them passionately. This everyday neurosis, which is perfectly compatible with an open and creative social life, is the result of an insufficient desexualization of the Oedipal parents. These childhood fantasms of poorly repressed pleasure and anxiety have preserved all of their virulence and generate this everyday neurosis that troubles all of us.

The other kind of neurotic trouble is, on the contrary, a *morbid* and *pathological* neurosis that is manifest in recurrent symptoms enclosing the subject in an unhealthy narcissistic solitude. This suffering, whether phobic, obsessional, or hysterical, is provoked by a factor that is more serious than the insufficient repression of the Oedipal fantasms. It is a question of the singular traumas experienced in the Oedipal period. What traumas? The first trauma, of a real or imaginary *abandonment*, strikes the child as an immense distress. This childhood fantasm of abandonment will lead to an adult phobia. Another possible trauma is that of a real or imaginary mistreatment, which inflicts a painful humiliation on the child. This fantasm of *mistreatment* and humiliation will lead to *obsession*. Finally, a third trauma, which is the most surprising, is the one in which the child experiences a suffocating pleasure during an overly sensual contact with an adult on which he or she depends. This fantasm of seduction will lead to *hysteria*. Whether it is the distress of being abandoned, the humiliation of mistreatment, or the suffocation linked to seduction, we are always in the presence of castration anxiety in its most morbid form, which borders on a *terror of castration*. We claim that phobia, obsession, and hysteria are different modes of the return of the traumatic Oedipus at an adult age. I would add that these three categories of neurosis never appear as isolated or pure, but are imbricated in a mixed neurosis of phobia, obsession, or hysteria. Further, these Oedipal traumas have at times been experienced not by the child itself but by an adult who has unconsciously transmitted the anxiety of a traumatic shock to him or her. A woman suffering from chronic agoraphobia, for example, insists that she was never abandoned in her childhood, but discovers, through psychoanalysis, that her mother had been traumatically abandoned during the war as a little girl. This is a case in which a transgenerational transmission of a fantasm of abandonment generates a phobia.

A pathological neurosis, then, in a man or a woman, is the return, at an adult age, of the traumatizing castration anxiety that was experienced during childhood. According to the mode of return of such an anxiety, a specific neurotic suffering will emerge (see Diagram 4). In clinical terms, if we are in the presence of a phobic patient, we must investigate his or her childhood in order to discover a possible incident in which he or she suffered anxiety as a result of a traumatic abandonment, whether this abandonment was real or imaginary. If our patient is a hysteric, we must look for another traumatic memory. In this case, the analysand recalls having been shocked, not by an abandonment but by another violence, much more subtle and insidious. He or she will recall having been captivated and excited by an adult seducer—father, mother, older brother, or friend of the family. With respect to this trauma, which is at the source of hysteria, see pages 80–81, and particularly Diagram 6. Finally, if we receive an obsessional patient, we must always seek a memory, a memory that reveals a powerless and enraged child, fearing the father's reprisals for a fault of which he is unaware. Briefly, whether it is a question of phobia, a hysteria, or an obsession, the suffering of a neurotic can be explained by his or her need to compulsively repeat the same situation in which he or she suffered the impact of a traumatic anxiety. In other words, neurosis is the compulsive return of an infantile fantasm of castration anxiety.

Thus, let us conclude that in the case of the masculine neurosis, *phobia* is the return, at an adult age, of the fantasm of the anxiety of being *abandoned* by a *prohibiting father*; that *hysteria* is the return of a fantasm of the anxiety of being *abused* by a *seductive father*; finally, that *obsession* is the return of the fantasm of the anxiety of being *mistreated and humiliated* by the *rival father* (Diagram 4). One sees that it is always the father who is the principal character of the traumatic fantasms at the source of the three masculine neuroses. Indeed, a man's neurosis, and as we will see, a woman's as well, results from the fixation of a scene where the principal character is often the parent of the *same* sex. Whether Oedipus is badly resolved or traumatic, the childhood conflict that causes the neurosis most often takes place between the boy and the father, or between the girl and the mother. What makes one sick is not so much an intense experience with another, but an experience with a similar other, another "oneself." The neurosis of the adult is always a pathology of the same, a sickness of narcissism. A young patient confided to me, for instance, "I suffer from being torn between the love for my father, the desire to resemble him, the desire to please him, the fear of becoming pitiful, the hatred that I have for him, and, finally, my revolt against his authority." Here is the cry of a neurotic son who suffers from being fascinated and horrified by the image of his father that is so close to his own.

The Reactivation of the Traumatic Oedipus in the Form of a Feminine Neurosis: Sexual Disgust, Masculinity Complex, and Anxiety of Being Abandoned

Let us consider now the case of the neurotic woman. Once the Oedipal crisis is overcome, should we conclude that the little girl has become pacified, without the shadow of a neurosis, free from any remaining traces of the past pain and her jealous envy? Certainly not. The life of a woman remains generally agitated by the persistence of former Oedipal conflicts. We can say already that of all the childhood passions that subsist in the life of the woman, the most disturbing, without doubt, is the jealous envy of the Phallus. In the case where this envy has been experienced in an overly agitated way in childhood, it can resurge violently in adulthood and manifest itself either as a hysterical sexual disgust, or as a pathological attitude known as the "masculinity complex." In the case of hysteria, the woman continues to believe, like a little girl, that she is not worthy of interest or love and resigns herself to her fate with bitterness and sadness. A strong disgust for sexuality coupled with a great solitude is thus established in this frustrated woman. In the case of the masculinity complex, on the contrary, the woman substitutes, in the place of the belief of being castrated and inferior, the opposite and equally unfounded belief of being armed with the Phallus. Instead of believing herself to be castrated, she believes herself to be omnipotent: she brandishes the Phallus, wields it defiantly, and accentuates masculine features to the point of being more masculine than the man. One of the variations of this masculinity complex takes the form of open homosexuality. Let us note in passing that the hypertrophy of masculinity in the woman can appear as one of the most tenacious resistances to therapeutic work and become the rock on which the psychoanalytic treatment often fails. The hateful rivalry with respect to men can be transformed in the analysand as a revolt against the supposed arbitrary male authority of the psychoanalyst.

I would like to add finally another Oedipal variation of the feminine neurosis, a variation that is close to normalcy. It is the question of *anxiety*:

a properly feminine anxiety. I have said that anxiety was prevalent in the masculine position and that the pain of privation characterized, rather, the feminine position. However, there is a typically feminine anxiety that I consider to be a form of castration anxiety, namely, the woman's fear of *being abandoned* by the man she loves. The desire to be loved and protected is so powerful in the feminine unconscious that the young woman, however fully involved in a committed relationship, always fears being deprived of the love of her companion. At the least conflict, she suspects her partner of wanting to leave her. As a little girl, she had been already deceived by her mother, and now that she is a woman she does not trust men. She fears losing the thing she held above all else: love, the joy of loving, of being loved and feeling protected. If, for the man, the Phallus is a force, for the woman, it is the happiness of being in love and of being loved by the one that she loves. **For the man, the Phallus is power; for the woman, it is love.** In the same way we said earlier that man was a being who is anxious to protect his virility, we would say that the woman is haunted by the fear of being abandoned. This is how, for the anxious woman, love remains a fragile achievement, always needing to be reconquered and confirmed (see Diagram 5 and Diagram 8).

I can imagine now the union of the neurotic man and woman, the one in the masculine position fearing that the woman will steal his sex from him (castration anxiety) and the other in the female position fearing that the man will abandon her (anxiety of being abandoned). Does this description reduce the man/woman couple to a revivification of Oedipal anxieties? The man worried about losing his virility and the woman anxious about losing love? Certainly not, since each demonstrates to the other by his or her presence that the anxiety is not justified. The man who is sincerely involved in his couple reassures his companion through the authenticity of his speech and actions, and the woman, who is just as sincerely engaged, assures her companion that apart from some difficulty, she will always confirm his virility. In this way the relation between a man and a woman should be able to unfold. And nevertheless, experience teaches us that between this ideal configuration and the staggering failure of the couple, every nuance is possible.

Now, I am going to discuss the clinical vignette of a hysterical patient suffering from anorexia, and whose body is consumed by her unconscious envy of the Phallus.

How Does One Listen to an Anorexic through the Prism of the Theory of the Oedipus Complex? Here Is My Hypothesis: Anorexia Results from the Identification of the Sick Young Woman with Her Brother, who is Idealized as Being the Preferred Son of the Father

Let us recall Sarah, an anorexic patient I spoke of just now. Against all reason, she wanted to attain the almost fatal threshold of forty-one kilos. "You will see," she boasted, "I can live without returning to the hospital! I bet you! I need to prove to myself that I can stand on a tightrope over an abyss." This was the madness of Sarah. It was mad challenge at the limits of life and a blind will to dominate and master her body. How is Oedipus operating here? How can the theory of Oedipus, as I conceive it, permit us to understand the suffering of this young woman? Well, when I receive this patient, I always think that she wants to become pure and light, almost evanescent, by erasing all the curves and feminine shape of her body. She no longer wishes to have breasts, buttocks, or even less, a stomach. No contours: nothing which would evoke a woman. Her dream is to become a beardless boy without a penis or any sign of virility. This ideal of a slender and fragile asexual man that she would like to be is none other, in her fantasm, than the marvelous son that her father dreamt of seducing and possessing sexually. Yes, she wishes to be the young (male) lover of the father, that is to say, to take the place of her adored brother, the favorite of the father. Sarah identifies then with the masculinity of her brother and refuses to be a woman because she thinks, like a four-year-old girl, that being a woman is equivalent to being castrated, weak, and despised by a father who would only have eyes for his son. Sarah believes, falsely, that the woman is castrated and that, consequently, she must do everything, to the point of risking her life, to show herself and the world that she is strong and that her body can be molded into the shape of a young man without genital organs. Our patient is in the grasp of Phallus envy, which is expressed here by her mad and jealous envy of being at the same time a boy with the masculine desire of possessing and mastering, and a girl having the feminine desire of being possessed by the father. Her anorexia is the expression of a compromise between these two unconscious impulses. I would like to say this in another way by formulating the following hypothesis: *anorexia is most often the result of the young girl's unconscious identification with her brother, a brother idealized as the favorite of the father.* In this hypothesis it could be a question of a virtual brother, or a masculine alter ego, since anorexics, obviously, do not all have brothers.

Commentary Concerning Diagram 4

There are two considerations to ponder. The first concerns the protagonists in play. It is immaterial whether the anguished child is a boy or a girl or whether the threatening adult (prohibitor, seducer or rival) is the father, the mother, the older brother, the older sister, or any other adult figure. However, the fantasm of castration anxiety that is most frequently encountered in the psychoanalytic treatment of neurotic men is that of a scene in which the child is a boy and the adult his father. For neurotic women, we find the same type of fantasm in which the girl fears the mother's reprisals. Also, the content of these fantasms is often a scene where the child is in relation to the parent of the same sex.

I would like to provide an example of a phobia. I am thinking of the case of a woman with the phobia of public transportation. Her analysis revealed that the cause of her neurosis was a tragic event in her childhood: the accidental death of her mother. Instead of experiencing the pain of mourning, as any child would have, she fantasized this death as an unexpected punishment inflicted by her loved and deceased mother. It was in this way that she became afraid of being abandoned again, a fear that had become a phobia of enclosed spaces.

The other consideration concerns a reading between the two columns of the table. It can be the case for example, that the anxiety of being abandoned by the prohibiting father, will reappear in the form of an obsessional neurosis that is no longer phobic, or that the anxiety of having been seduced but an overly affectionate parent is the source of a phobic neurosis that is no longer hysterical.

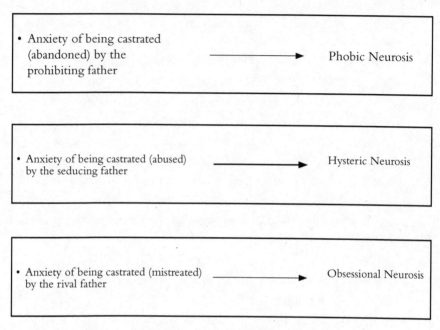

Fantasm of Castration Anxiety

The Neurosis is the compulsive reappearance of the traumatic Fantasm of Castration Anxiety at an adult age

- Anxiety of being castrated (abandoned) by the prohibiting father → Phobic Neurosis

- Anxiety of being castrated (abused) by the seducing father → Hysteric Neurosis

- Anxiety of being castrated (mistreated) by the rival father → Obsessional Neurosis

Diagram 4 The morbid neurosis proper to men entails the compulsive reappearance of the trauma of Oedipus in adulthood.

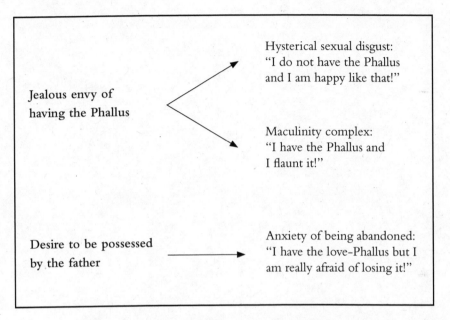

Fantasm of the jealous envy of the Phallus

Neurosis is the compulsive reappearance of the Fantasm of the jealous envy of the Phallus in adulthood

Jealous envy of
having the Phallus

Hysterical sexual disgust:
"I do not have the Phallus
and I am happy like that!"

Maculinity complex:
"I have the Phallus and
I flaunt it!"

Desire to be possessed
by the father

Anxiety of being abandoned:
"I have the love-Phallus but I
am really afraid of losing it!"

Diagram 5   The morbid neurosis proper to women
is due to the compulsive reappearance of traumatic Oedipus in adulthood.

Archipelago of Oedipus

Castration Does not Exist! There Is No Castration, There Are Only Threats of Castration. This Is Why Castration, in the Final Analysis, Is Nothing but the Name of an Anxiety, and Never of a Reality

From the beginning we have constantly used the word *castration* without having had the opportunity to dissipate a possible misunderstanding with respect to its meaning. I would like to address this now. First, let us state clearly that, apart from certain isolated barbaric acts, castration does not exist, and that no one has ever been castrated and certainly not castrated as a punishment! Of course, we know of the "chemical" castrations whose aim is to treat, as a last resort, certain perverse cases such as rapists and pedophiles. And we know also that certain psychotic patients commit sexual self-mutilation or castrate a victim. But apart from these psychopathological aberrations, I insist that castration properly speaking does not exist. If Freud provided this suggestive term, it was in order to dramatize, indeed render hysterical, the imaginary danger that threatens all men and all women who desire, that is to say, all men and all women who ardently seek corporeal pleasure, and beyond that . . . happiness. What danger threatens them? The danger of losing their vitality, their life, the intimate source of their desire. What, then, is castration? Castration is above all the idea of a danger, the imaginary danger invented by a neurotic, a danger that he or she must necessarily avoid. It is by wishing to protect his or her vital being and by being constantly on the lookout that the neurotic suffers from being neurotic. Consequently, it is always the *fear* of castration and never castration itself that is the source of this tension of neurotic suffering. Each neurotic symptom is thus to be understood as an anxious defense against an essential fear: the man's fear of losing his power and the woman's fear of losing her love. Also, the word "castration" is an incomparable psychoanalytic allegory that symbolizes the hypothetical loss of a hypothetical supreme object.

One understands henceforth that, for Freud, each of us is, in the final analysis, a desirous and voracious child, fearful when faced with the consequences of his immoderate desire, jealous guardian of his Phallus, and feeling guilty of desiring. Voracious, fearful, jealous, and guilty: this is the most intimate and accurate portrait that Freud has painted of us with the colors of Oedipus.

The Figures of the Father in the Masculine Oedipus

The father is loved as an ideal model
The father is feared as a prohibitor and a censor
The father is desired and feared as a seducer
The father is hated and feared as a rival

The love of the boy for the father he admires existed well before his entry into the Oedipal crisis. The feelings of filial tenderness and admiration persist throughout the Oedipus period and meet other opposing feelings, including desire, anxiety, and hatred. It is precisely the simultaneous experience of all these contradictory feelings that divide the child and foment his neurosis. The neurotic, whether a child or an adult, is the one who loves, fears, desires, and hates the father simultaneously.

The Figures of the Mother in the Feminine Oedipus

In the *Pre-Oedipal* stage:

The all-powerful mother equipped with the Phallus (phallic mother) is loved as an ideal figure.
The mother is desired as a sexual object that the girl wants to possess. For the child not only does the mother have the Phallus but she is the Phallus.

In the stage of *Solitude*:

The mother is blamed by her daughter for having been incapable of giving her the Phallus, the symbol of power.
The mother is thus stripped of all her power and abandoned.

In the *Oedipal* stage:

> The mother, as a woman desiring a man, is a model of
> identification.
> The mother is loved once again, but this time as a feminine ideal.
> The mother is hated as a rival.

The Figures of the Phallus in the Feminine Oedipus

In the eyes of the little girl, the Phallus takes on different forms in the
course of the successive stages of her Oedipus.

> In the pre-Oedipal stage, the little girl recognizes the Phallus in her
> clitoral sensations and in the person of her mother, considered
> as the chosen object of her desire. The Phallus is thus here
> incarnated by the Clitoris as an organ of erogenous sensations,
> and by the Mother as an object of incestuous desire.
> In the stage of Solitude she recognizes the phallus in the fascinating
> penis of the boy, and conscious of her privation, she recognizes
> it painfully in her wounded self-image. The Phallus is thus
> incarnated by penis envy of the boy and the self-image.
> In the Oedipus stage the Phallus is incarnated by the Force of the
> father, a force that the girl covets, and later, after the first paternal
> refusal, is incarnated by Herself as an object that she offers the
> father. Finally, for the daughter, after the second paternal refusal,
> the Phallus becomes her introjected Father.
> Having overcome her Oedipus complex, the little girl, who has
> now become a woman, will recognize the Phallus in the erect
> Penis of the man she loves, in the Love that this man has for her,
> and finally in the Child that is the fruit of this love.

The erogenous sensations, the Mother, the boy's Penis, the Self-Image,
the Force of the father, oneself, the figure of the Father, the erect penis
of the man she loves, Love and the Child, are all avatars of the feminine
Oedipus. Each of these avatars corresponds precisely to the definition of

the Phallus not only as the most valuable thing but also as the vital and irreplaceable regulator of our psychical equilibrium.

The Super-Ego and the Three Roles of the Father in the Masculine Oedipus

The super-ego, that self-critical part of the self, that part of the ego that censors the ego, is an agency that reactivates three contradictory attitudes of the fantasmatic father in the psyche. Also, the super-ego is a choir of three voices: the severe voice of the prohibition that presents the *prohibiting father*, the persuasive voice of temptation that presents the *seductive father*, and the denigrating voice of self-reproach that presents the *hated and rival father*.

Playing with Dolls

The little Oedipal girl has the doll play two different roles. In the pre-Oedipal stage, the little girl repeats the relation with her mother with her doll. She identifies with the doll and at the same time she identifies with the mother by cuddling. Once she enters the Oedipal complex, strictly speaking, the little girl changes roles. Now the girl is the mother and the doll is the marvelous child that the father has given her.

The Fantasm of Phallic Omnipotence

In the mind of Oedipal children, those who have the Phallus are strong and those who do not have the Phallus are weak. Obviously, such a fiction that takes the penis to be synonymous with power, and its absence with weakness, is a cartoon imagined by four-year-olds and in no way an adult thought. Nevertheless, this childhood fiction can persist in adulthood as a mirage that creates conflict between the neurotic with both himself and those around him. Thus, the neurotic perceives those who matter to him according to a Manichean vision distinguishing between the strong and the weak, between the dominant and the dominated.

Phobia Is a Projection, Hysteria a Rebellion, and Obsession a Displacement

Let us shift the perspective and explain the presence of Oedipus in the three neuroses by having recourse to metapsychology. Hence, we will say that *phobia* results from the *projection* of castration anxiety on the external world. Unconscious anxiety becomes conscious fear. The internal danger, represented by the prohibiting father, is projected outside and becomes an external danger that is incarnated, for example, by animals. Freud gave us an eloquent illustration of this in the well-known case of Little Hans. The frightening horse is the father and the fear of the horses is a symptom of the fear of being mutilated and abandoned by the father. In a word, phobia can be defined as the projection of an internal danger outside, thus becoming an external danger—as the substitution of the fantasmatic threatening father by a threatening animal (that exists in reality)—and finally as the transformation of an unconscious anxiety into a conscious fear.

Setting aside *conversion hysteria*, which results from the *concentration* of the entire charge of unconscious anxiety in the body, provoking thus a somatic dysfunction (migraine, vertigo, pain, etc.), I recognize another form of hysteria that is much more insidious and common, which I call the *hysteria of rebellion*. This neurosis is brought about by the resurgence, in the adult, of the childhood anxiety of being seduced by one of the parents, in particular the parent of the same sex. Among the childhood fantasms of anxiety, the most pathogenic is the one of a scene where the boy, seduced but also frightened, plays the role of a female possessed by his father. If such a fantasm remains active in the unconscious of the hysterical man, it will manifest itself by a reaction of permanent revolt. For example, whenever he finds himself in a normal dependent relation with an other who is admired or is an authority, the hysteric feels oppressed, subjected, and—according to his fantasms—almost relegated to the rank of a castrated female [*femmelette châtrée*] who is "tyrannized." For him, being dependent means "being a woman" because in his fantasm the woman is a weak being, inferior to the man and, in the end, negligible. Thus, dependence on an authority will be experienced by the neurotic as the worst of submissions, and, consequently, as the most urgent necessity to rebel and protect his self-esteem. It is in this way that the person who incarnates the authority becomes, in his eyes, a despot who must be overthrown.

When a patient adopts such a hysterical position, it is extremely difficult for us as psychoanalysts, to reveal his fantasm of unconscious seduction to the analysand, and even more so to resolve it. Why? Because the psychoanalyst, like the father, becomes for that patient a redoubtable seducer, and therefore, an authority to depose. If this transferential figure becomes dominant, the cure risks being brutally interrupted. The childhood fantasm of seduction can invade the psychoanalytic relation to such an extent that any intervention by the practitioner will be systematically interpreted by the analysand as an intolerable abuse of power. Freud, the first, ran aground on this impassable obstacle that he called "the rock of castration." Rather, I would say, "the rock of the *anxiety* of castration," since what nourishes the vehement rebellion of the neurotic against the psychoanalyst is nothing other than the anxiety of being the slave of the father, and of losing his human dignity. By rebelling, the hysteric believes he will save his Phallus, which he never had, from the hands of a tyrant that the psychoanalyst has never been.

Let us add in passing that we can suffer the same failure in the treatment of a woman when the analysand, embittered, criticizes her psychoanalyst for his arrogance and chauvinism. This kind of reaction comes from a jealous envy with respect to the therapist who she assumes to bear the Phallus, that is to say, that she supposes to be powerful, always happy, loved and admired by everyone. Frustrated and furious, she would also like to be endowed with the same magical force, indeed, to be stronger than he, to make him weak and become his only recourse. Whereas the man interrupts his treatment because of the fear of being like a woman, the woman, for her part, stops treatment out of rage and frustration. As the man's rock of castration is distinguished by anxiety, the woman's is distinguished by jealous envy. In both cases, *neurotic men and women have a devalued image of the woman, and an overestimation of the Phallus.* The neurotic man does not understand that the Phallus that he safeguards jealously is a nonexistent object and that therefore there is no risk of losing something that does not exist! There is no reason to be afraid since there is no danger or threat. The neurotic woman, for her part, does not understand that the Phallus is a delusion and that she has no reason to fight with the man for an object that he does not have.

Obsession results from a *displacement* of the castration anxiety that passes from the unconscious to the conscious and crystallizes in a feeling of guilt. The unconscious anxiety of being beaten by the rival father transforms into the conscious anxiety of being punished by one's own super-ego. This anxiety of feeling at fault and liable to be punished is called a feeling of guilt. It often happens that the obsessional finds pleasure in his or her role as guilty, needs to be punished and exhaust him or herself in a sterile *jouissance* known as moral masochism.

The Bisexual Signification of a Neurotic Symptom

Faced with a neurotic symptom, the psychoanalyst must attempt to reveal the fantasmatic scene that was forged long ago in Oedipal childhood and that governs the neurosis today. In this situation the subject plays a double role, active and passive, or to be more exact, it enacts a conflict between two characters that it plays: one, a dominant masculine character, and another, a dominated feminine character. Thus, when you are faced with a patient suffering from a phobia of flying, for example, you should know that the fantasmatic scene that fuels the anxiety is played by an oppressive father—the closed space of the airplane—and by a threatened child—the phobic himself. Let me emphasize further that in the fantasm, the subject plays the two roles simultaneously: it is both the virile tormenter and the effeminate victim, both the oppressive father as the powerless child. Clearly, it is above all the latter role that the neurotic prefers.

What Is Hysteria?

I have said that Oedipus is an excess. It is a sexual desire, evocative of an adult sexual desire, present in the little mind and the little body of a four-year-old child, and whose parents are the object. Inversely, I would say that *hysteria* is an *infantile* sexual desire experienced in the head of an *adult* and whose object is not a man or a woman but a person who is strong or weak. The hysteric experiences his or her partner not as a man or a woman but as a person who is castrated or all-powerful.

The Hysteria Suffered by an Adult Was Provoked by an Overly Sensual Relation between the Child He or She Was and the Parents

Here is what Oedipus teaches us: the hysteria that afflicts an adult was provoked long ago by a violent shock experienced in his or her childhood sexuality. In effect, it is a disturbance in the child's sexual life that is the source of current neurotic torments. What sort of disturbance? What happened to the little Oedipal child such that a neurosis is henceforth established in the adult? Well, a loss of control has occurred. Yes, the Oedipal child suffered from having been overwhelmed by an overly intense sexual pleasure that overtook him or her. His or her ego, still inexperienced, was unable to manage the impetuosity of uncontrollable desire and unable to assimilate the excessive pleasure that resulted from it. Was this desire or pleasure? They are perfectly equivalent since, as we have seen, sensations, desire, fantasms, and pleasure are experienced by the Oedipal child as one and the same thing. We are the ones who differentiate the elements. That being said, when erogenous pleasure is excessive the child's ego is traumatized. In other words—and this is the great lesson of Oedipus—when the ego of the child is incapable of integrating the destabilizing impact of sexual pleasure, it is distraught and condemned to relive the same trauma over and over again. I would like to insist moreover that such a phenomenon is astonishing. For it is the pleasure and not the pain, as one might believe, that makes the Oedipal child and future hysteric suffer. It is not only the pain that is traumatic—an excessive sexual pleasure can also be painful.

This is how the traumatizing gap between an immature ego and an intense and precocious pleasure makes its impression in the wax of the child's unconscious. Like a sensitive plate, the unconscious preserves the brutal shock of erogenous pleasure along with context in memory, that is, the sensual and desiring presence of the adult. There is no traumatic sexual pleasure that is not triggered by the excitation, whether innocent or not, that comes from one of the parents. This is how the prototype of a fantasmatic scene in which the child is seduced by one of the parents is molded in his or her virginal unconscious. Much later, as an adult, the subject experiences—and this is the neurosis—the compulsive need to relive the same sensation of that painful pleasure to replay the same traumatic scene, this time not with the parents but with the current partner. To state this clearly: *The traumatic experience of undergoing overwhelming sexual sensations can be, for a child, the source of a future neurosis.* By way of conclusion, I would like to outline the sequence of the formation of a neurosis. We have a precondition and three stages. The precondition is the immaturity of the child, the anachronism of a sexual pleasure that is too intense for a little four-year-old child. It is then that the trauma (first stage) is crystallized in a fantasmatic scene of pleasure and pain (second stage). The scene that perpetuates the trauma is replayed endlessly by the subject in his or her adult life (third stage). And that is the neurosis!

The Hysterical Woman and Her Fear of Love

The fantasmatic scene into which the child is drawn, excited and finally abused by an adult-seducer, constitutes one of the fantasms most frequently encountered in the treatment of hysterical patients, whether men or women. Concerning the woman, the fantasm of seduction is often the cause of difficulties in her love life. She desires to be loved by a man, and at the same time she is afraid he will suffocate her, or on the contrary that he will abandon her. For a hysteric, all suitors are perceived through the murky fog of a childhood fantasm of seduction: "They are all the same! Good talkers! Once they have what they want, they will leave me!" The childhood anxiety of being submitted to the father has become in the hysteric a rebellion against all men on whom she could depend. And the anxiety of being abandoned has become a phobia of love.

The Three Lacanian Figures of the Father in the Oedipus Complex: Symbolic, Real, and Imaginary

My view is that Lacan analyzes the process of Oedipus in three stages according to the following principle, namely, the different roles that the child has the father play in its Oedipal fantasms. During the first stage of Oedipus, the father is not incarnated. He is the abstract figure of the Law protecting the human world from the chaos that would ensue with the commission of incest. This eminently abstract father, a safeguard against the madness of man and represented by human language, is called the *symbolic father*. In the first stage the father is the tacit Law of which the child is unaware. Without restraint or fear the child impudently seduces his mother and offers himself to her as being her Phallus. In the second stage it is the real person of the father that matters. The father is now the *real father*, a divisive force that separates mother and child and forbids each from taking the other as an object of desire. It is in the third stage that the child confronts the divisive and frustrating father by respecting him as all-powerful, by hating him as a rival, and by being jealous of him as the one who possesses the Phallus. That is to say, as the sole possessor of the mother, of all women, and of power. This father, who is respected, hated and envied, is the *imaginary father*. It is from him that the child will demand the Phallus in vain. Of course, the father refuses and this refusal immediately entails the identification of the son with the father, synthesizing thus the three paternal figures: symbolic, real, and imaginary. Since the child cannot have the object, he identifies with the one who possesses the object.

In sum, the Oedipal child encounters three paternal characters. First, the father is the structure of the Law ruling the society in which he is born; then, the father is the policeman who enforces the Law; finally, the father is still the policeman, but feared as an authority, challenged as a power, and envied as one who is all-powerful. It is as if, in the first act of a puppet show of Oedipus, the insolent little boy tried to sway his mother by whispering, "Take me to you! No one can see us," and as if, in the second act, one suddenly saw the policeman leap from his box and scream: "What are you two doing! Stop immediately!"; and finally, in the third act, it is as if the contrite and admiring boy respectfully asked the policeman if he could borrow his baton in order to someday become as strong as him. Faced with refusal, the child gives in, incorporates the figure of authority, and, dividing himself, becomes at times the rebel, and at times the policeman who represses the rebel. Henceforth, this little scene with two characters, one who transgresses and the other who punishes, will dominate affective life as a whole, the crucial actions and situations that highlight the existence of a subject. In a word, the experience of the Oedipus complex can be read as the encounter of a child with the three figures of the father—symbolic, real, and imaginary—a father who represents the *Law*, an other who enforces it, and finally the one, envied and contested, who holds the *Power*. These are the three introjected paternal figures that together will form the boy's super-ego.

ADULT NEUROSIS (REPETITION COMPULSION	Once an adult, the subject experiences the compulsive need of reliving the same sensation of pleasure that caused it pain, and of replaying the same traumatic scene this time no longer including the parents, but its current partners
FIXATION OF THE TRAUMA IN A FANTASMATIC SCENE THAT HAS BECOME PATHOGENIC	Like a sensitive photographic plate, the unconscious of the child registers the brutal impact of erogenous pleasure associated with the sensual presence of the adult. This is how the picture of the fantasmatic scene seduction by one of the parents is printed in the unconscious.

PSYCHICAL TRAUMA

TRAUMATIZING SEXUAL PLEASURE IN THE OEDIPAL CHILD	THE GAP BETWEEN SEXUAL PLEASURE AND THE CHILD'S EGO On the one hand, an intense, burning, erogenous pleasure, triggered in the child by a desiring adult and on whom the child depends; on the other hand, an infantile ego that is stupefied and incapable of integrating this overwhelming pleasure mentally. This is a problem of excess and of temporal asymmetry: the pleasure is too strong and it comes too early

Diagram 6   Hysteria suffered by an adult was provoked by an overly sensual relation between the child that he or she was and the parents. A child's premature experience of an erogenous pleasure can be just as traumatic as a pain.

Commentary on the chart
on three types of lack in Oedipus

Castration is an idea; privation a fact; and frustration a demand refused. For the boy, castration is an idea that produces anxiety, the idea that he can lack what is for him most crucial; while for the girl, privation is a painful fact, the fact that she lacks something crucial that she thought she had. With respect to frustration, for the girl, it is the disappointment that follows the father's refusal to take her as phallus. Disappointed, she struggles nevertheless to obtain the two main forms of the Phallus in the life of a woman: to love and to conceive a child with the man she loves.

INCESTUOUS DESIRE	PHALLUS: PRECIOUS OBJECT	TYPE OF LACK	AGENT OF THE LACK	EXPERIENCE OF THE LACK
THE OEDIPAL DESIRE OF THE BOY TO POSSESS HIS MOTHER	I fear losing . . . an object I thought I had: the imaginary Phallus	The lack is an idea: Castration is Symbolic	The agent of Castration is the prohibiting, seductive, and rival father	**Anxiety** of losing my Phallus-penis, my Phallus-virility, or my Phallus-power
THE PREOEDIPAL DESIRE OF THE GIRL TO POSSESS HER MOTHER	I have lost... an object I believed I had: the symbolic Phallus	The lack is a fact: **the Privation is Real**	The agent of privation is The deficient mother	**The pain of** Privation
THE OEDIPAL DESIRE OF THE GIRL TO BE POSSESSED BY HER FATHER	I want to be... the precious object of my father: the **real** Phallus	The lack is a disappoint-ment: **Frustration is Imaginary**	The agent of frustration is the **father** who refuses to take his daughter as the **Phallus**	The daughter does not give up and **fights** to become woman and mother

Diagram 7   Three types of lack in Oedipus: castration, privation, and frustration. A Reading of the Lacanian triad.

In the experience of Oedipus, the child experiences, for the first time, desires that determine its future sexual identity: the masculine desire to possess, and the feminine desire to be possessed. Here is a chart comparing the masculine and feminine positions. Of course these two positions can be occupied interchangeably by a man or a woman. There are numerous women who desire according to the masculine type, and numerous men who desire according to the feminine type. "Masculine" and "feminine" are words that designate dominant psychical positions; it is impossible, and this is for the better, to psychoanalytically define the perfect type of man or woman, since the particularities are infinite

DOMAINS	MASCULINE POSITION	FEMININE POSITION
Oedipal Desire	The desire to possess	The desire to be possessed
Sexuality	• The man is sexually hyperactive, proud of his sex, and desirous of giving the woman *jouissance*. • In a centrifugal movement, a man wants to protect, contain, and *penetrate* the loved woman. • A man can love a woman, and without renouncing that love, desire another. Love and sex are disassociated.	• Unlike a man, a woman is particularly sensitive to *the quality* of the sexual relation. • In a centripetal movement, woman wants to be protected, be contained, and receive the sex of the man loved. For a woman, to offer oneself does not mean to be passive or submissive. • A woman's erogenous sensitivity is more rich and varied than a man's, which remains focused on his penis. • A fullfilled woman loves a man who satisfies her sexually. Love and sex are indissociable.
Behavior toward the loved partner	• A man prefers loving to being loved. • He idealizes the loved woman and effaces himself before her. The humility of the amorous man.	• The woman prefers to be loved by the man that she loves. She always needs to be reassured.

Diagram 8

DOMAINS	MASCULINE POSITION	FEMININE POSITION
Narcissism	• Narcissism of doing the good rather than of being handsome. For a man it is more important to be strong than handsome.	• Narcissism of feeling beautiful rather than appearing beautiful. For a woman it is more important to be indispensable than to be powerful. She wants to be the only one.
Power/ Powerlessness	• The alternative between being strong or weak is of vital concern for a man.	• Being strong or weak is not her problem. The concern of a woman is to be loved and not be abandoned.
Determination and Courage	• Man, essentially a coward, delays making a commitment, judges the risks, hesitates, and recoils before the act.	• Once she decides to commit, the woman shows courage and unshakable determination.
Social Attitude	• A man tends to boast of his power.	• A woman prefers to ignore her power and occupy herself with her intimate feelings.
Will	• Great will, foresight, and perseverance in action.	• Fierce determination to conquer love and protect her child.
Why are the masculine and feminine positions different?	• Man is endowed with a detachable appendage, the penis that symbolizes everything that he fears losing: his power and his virility. The fear of losing his strength is so embedded in the mind of man that for him any act is a risk and any failure, a humiliation. • The supreme dangers for a man are the vindictive woman and the admired father.	• In her imaginary, a woman does not possess an appendage to manipulate or safeguard, but an invisible object: that must be her most precious treasure: to love and be loved. She has nothing to lose except love. For her, love is a permanent conquest, a good to be constantly reconquered. Any action, even that risks her life, is, to be sure, an action that scares her, but she is much more confident than a man. She knows what man forgets: there are no definitive achievements.

Diagram 8 (continued)

Excerpts from the Work of Sigmund Freud and Jacques Lacan on Oedipus Preceded by Our Commentary

(The headings and the passages in bold font that introduce the excerpts from Freud and Lacan are provided by Dr. Nasio.)

Freud

THE UNIVERSALITY OF THE OEDIPUS COMPLEX

All children, whatever their familial and sociocultural conditions might be, experience the universal fantasm of the Oedipus complex. Whether the child of a classic, recomposed, or single parent family, or else a child of a homosexual couple, or even an abandoned, orphaned, or adopted child, no child escapes Oedipus! Why? Because no child escapes from the flood of the drives raging within him or her when they are about three or four years old, and because no adult of his or her immediate surroundings can avoid playing the role of the target of these drives and of a conduit in which to channel them.

[A] still higher degree of interest must attach to the influence of a situation which *every child* is destined to pass through and which follows inevitably from the factor of the prolonged period during which a child is cared for by other people and lives with his parents.

I am thinking of the *Oedipus complex*, so named because its essential
substance is to be found in the Greek legend of King Oedipus....
The Greek hero killed his father and took his mother to wife ...
unwittingly.... [1]

At this point the boy had to fit into a phylogenetic pattern, and
he did so, although his personal experiences may not have agreed
with it.[2]

[The] phylogenetically inherited schemata ... are precipitates
from the history of human civilization. The Oedipus complex ... is
one of them.[3]

She stood under the domination of the Oedipus complex, even
though she did not know that this universal phantasy had in her
case become a reality.[4]

THE DISCOVERY OF THE OEDIPUS COMPLEX

**It is on the basis of childhood memories of a sexual nature
mentioned by our adult patients that we deduced the existence of
the Oedipus complex. Let us not forget that a memory is always a
very subjective reinterpretation of the past.**

My surprising discoveries as to the sexuality of children were made in the
first instance through the analysis of adults.[5]

Behind these phantasies there came to light the material which allows
us to draw the picture which follows of the development of the sexual
function.[6]

OEDIPUS WAS DISCOVERED BY FREUD ON THE BASIS OF THE NARRATION OF SEDUCTION SCENES THAT HIS ADULT PATIENTS BELIEVED THEY HAD EXPERIENCED IN THEIR CHILDHOOD

**The Oedipus complex is not a reality that can be observed
but a sexual fantasm forged by the child under the influence
of his or her incestuous desire. The contents of this fantasm**

are often a scene of sexual seduction by an adult. We note as well that the Oedipal fantasm, while created in childhood and always active in the neurotic adult, must be reconstructed by the analyst in the course of therapy. The analyst reconstructs it "on the spot" since the analyst/patient relation reenacts the Oedipal relation.

> I was at last obliged to recognize that these scenes of seduction had never taken place, and that they were only phantasies which my patients had made up . . . [7]

The memory of being sexually seduced by the father is one of the forms in which the Oedipus complex can present itself. The fantasm of seduction is only a version of the Oedipal fantasm. It takes but an overly tender gesture on the part of a parent (in general, the father) for the child to forge the memory of an ambiguous gesture of sexual seduction.

> Having recognized "these scenes of seduction . . . which my patients had made up . . . I had in fact stumbled for the first time upon the *Oedipus complex.*"[8]

INCESTUOUS DESIRE IS THE SOURCE OF ALL HUMAN DESIRES

Incestuous desire, not only cannot be realized, but is even inconceivable by a four-year-old child. However, it is this mythical desire, beyond and prior to any genital life, which we psychoanalysts assume to be the source of all human desires and fantasms.

> With boys the wish to beget a child from their mother is never absent, with girls the wish to have a child by their father is equally constant; and this is in spite of their being completely incapable of forming any clear idea of the means for fulfilling their wishes.[9]

INCESTUOUS DESIRE IS PARTIALLY SATISFIED IN A FANTASM

Being beaten by the father is a fantasm that partially satisfies the incestuous desire of a boy to be sexually possessed by his father. Physical pain then becomes sexual pleasure. In this respect, we note that a traumatic incident of significant physical violence, experienced in childhood or adolescence, can determine the sexually passive position (masochism) in a man with respect to a masculine or feminine partner who dominates and belittles him.

> The boy's beating-phantasy is therefore passive from the very beginning, and is derived from a feminine attitude toward his father.[10]

THE OEDIPUS OF THE BOY AND OF THE GIRL

The boy renounces his mother because he is afraid, while the girl deserts her mother who betrays her, and turns toward her father.

> In a boy the Oedipus complex, in which he desires his mother and would like to get rid of his father as being a rival, develops naturally from the phase of his phallic sexuality. The threat of castration compels him, however, to give up that attitude. Under the impression of the danger of losing his penis, the Oedipus complex is abandoned, repressed and, in the most normal cases, entirely destroyed, and a severe super-ego is set up as its heir.
>
> What happens with a girl is almost the opposite. The castration complex prepares for the Oedipus complex instead of destroying it; the girl is driven out of her attachment to her mother through the influence of her envy for the penis and she enters the Oedipus situation as though into a haven of refuge.[11]

THE THREE PHASES OF THE OEDIPUS COMPLEX FOR THE GIRL

According to our reading, the feminine Oedipus is divided into three stages. First, the pre-Oedipal stage, in which the girl, from a masculine position, desires her mother as a sexual object; second, the stage I call "pain of privation" in the course of which the girl is alone, mortified and jealous of the boy; and finally, third, the properly Oedipal stage in which the girl is inhabited by a feminine desire to be possessed by the father.

> Their sexual life is regularly divided into two phases, of which the first has a masculine character, while only the second is specifically feminine.[12]

Between the first and the second stage proposed by Freud, I insert an intermediary stage where the girl, alone and mortified, adopts a masculine position of rivalry.

THE SUPER-EGO IS OUR PSYCHICAL FATHER

Our super-ego can be very severe or quite lenient according to the rapidity and the violence of the repression of the Oedipus complex.

> The super-ego retains the character of the father, while the more powerful the Oedipus complex was and the more rapidly it succumbed to repression (under the influence of authority, religious teaching, schooling and reading), the stricter will be the domination of the super-ego over the ego later on—in the form of conscience or perhaps of an unconscious sense of guilt.[13]

NEUROSIS IS THE REACTIVATION
OF OEDIPUS AS AN ADULT

The Oedipus complex is the cause of neurosis because Oedipal fantasms, poorly repressed in childhood, reappear in the adult as neurotic symptoms. We can put it another way. The neurosis in an adult can be explained by the intensity with which he experienced sexual pleasure as a child, and by the violence or instability with which he repressed it.

> For this reason infantile sexuality, which is held under repression, acts as the chief motive force in the formation of symptoms; and the essential part of its content, the Oedipus complex, is the nuclear complex of neuroses.[14]

> For in our opinion the Oedipus complex is the actual nucleus of neuroses, and the infantile sexuality which culminates in this complex is the true determinant of neuroses. What remains of the complex in the unconscious represents the disposition to the later development of neuroses in the adult.[15]

> I was driven to recognize in the end that these reports were untrue and so came to understand that hysterical symptoms are derived from phantasies and not from real occurrences.[16]

Lacan

OEDIPUS IS A THEORY OF THE FAMILY

The theory of Oedipus is a theory of the family, and in particular, that of the social decline of the paternal image. It is precisely this decline of the role of the father that is the source of the neuroses.

The discovery that . . . sexual repression and psychical sex were subject to regulation and to the accidents of a psychical drama of the family, brought about the most precious collaboration with the anthropology of familial grouping . . . Freud also arrived quickly at a theory of the family. It was based on a asymmetry . . . in the situation of the two sexes in relation to Oedipus.[17]

We are not among those who bemoan an alleged weakening of the family bond. . . . But a significant number of psychological effects seem to indicate a social decline of the paternal imago. . . . This decline constitutes a psychological crisis. Perhaps the appearance of psychoanalysis itself was due to that crisis. The sublime chance of genius alone cannot explain what happened in Vienna . . . namely, that a son of the Jewish patriarchy imagined the Oedipus complex. Whatever the case may be, it was the dominant forms of neuroses at the end of the 19th century that revealed that they were intimately dependent on the conditions of the family.[18]

THE PHALLIC STAGE

In the Phallic stage, the child sexually desires one of the parents without engaging, of course, in any sexual act. In the place of nonexistent genitalia, a fantasm of possessing an all-powerful Phallus develops in the child.

Just before the period of latency, the infantile subject, masculine or feminine, reaches the phallic stage, which indicates the point of genital realization. Everything happens there, up to and including the choice of the object. However, there is something which is not yet accomplished, that is, the full realization of the genital function.

Indeed, there remains a fantasmatic, essentially imaginary, element, namely, the prevalence of the phallus, through which, there are for the subject two types of beings in the world—those who have the phallus and those who do not, that is to say, those who are castrated.[19]

THE OMNIPOTENCE OF THE MOTHER

Lacan opposed the idea that the child was inhabited by a feeling of omnipotence. Only the mother could wield omnipotence, since the child supposes it of her. There is only the omnipotence of the Other, and the very first castration experienced by a child is the anxious finding that the mother is as vulnerable as he or she is.

> It is wrong to think . . . that the child has the notion of his or her omnipotence. Not only does nothing indicate in his or her development that he or she has it, but . . . his or her alleged omnipotence and its failures are not at issue. What matters . . . are the deficiencies, and the disappointments that affect maternal omnipotence.[20]

THE FATHER IS A METAPHOR

For Lacan, the father is the principal character of the Oedipal drama, whether in the masculine or the feminine Oedipus.

> There is no question of Oedipus if there is no father, and inversely, to speak of Oedipus is to introduce the function of the father as essential.[21]

In the Oedipus complex, the status of the father is metaphorical: it is the signifier that takes the place of another signifier. The signifier "father" takes the place of the signifier "desire of the mother." The father signifies the desire of the mother. In other words, for the child, the father is also a man, a man that the mother desires.

> What is the father? I do not mean in the context of the family. . . . The entire question is to determine his role in the

Oedipus complex. . . . It is this: the father is a metaphor. . . . the father is a signifier substituted for another signifier. This is the role, the essential role, the unique role of the intervention of the father in the Oedipus complex. . . . The function of the father in the Oedipus complex is to be a signifier substituted for the first signifier introduced by symbolization, the maternal signifier. . . . According to the definition . . . of metaphor, the father takes the place of the mother.[22]

IMAGINARY TRIAD, SYMBOLIC QUATUOR

For Lacan, the mother–child–Phallus triangle is an imaginary pre-Oedipal triad. Oedipus only appears with the introduction of a fourth element, the father. The imaginary triad thus becomes a symbolic quatuor. The passage from one to the other takes place through a disappointment: the child is disappointed to learn that it does not have the Phallus of the mother. It discovers that the object of desire of the mother is in the father and not in it. Accordingly, it is toward the father, keeper of the Phallus, that the child turns.

The dialectic of the three first objects [mother–child–phallus] and of the fourth term which encompasses them all and links them in the symbolic relation, is the father. This term introduces the symbolic relation.[23]

The imaginary mother–child–phallus triad, as a prelude to the opening of the symbolic relation, which only takes place with the fourth function, that of the father, introduced by the dimension of Oedipus. The triangle is in itself pre-Oedipal. . . . The quatuor . . . is constituted when the parental function enters the scene, on the basis of . . . the fundamental disappointment of the child. The child not only recognizes . . . that he or she is not the unique object of the mother, but that the mother's interest is the phallus. From this recognition, the child must realize, secondly, that the mother is precisely deprived, that she herself lacks that object.[24]

LACAN AND THE SYMBOLIC NATURE OF THE GIFT

Lacan emphasizes the symbolic nature of the gift, either the gift in the sense of demanding the object from the other, or the gift in the sense of giving the object to the other. The girl enters into Oedipus when she demands the Phallus from her father, the boy leaves Oedipus when—in order to save his penis—he resigns himself to relinquishing the object that he wanted so much, that is, his mother; he renounces his mother as an object of desire.

> It is insofar as the female child does not possess the phallus that she is introduced to the symbolic nature of the gift. It is insofar as . . . it is a matter of having or not having the phallus that she enters the Oedipus complex. The boy . . . does not enter the Oedipus complex in the same way, for it is from there that he exits. At the end of the Oedipus complex . . . he must give what he has.[25]

CASTRATION AND PRIVATION

Castration is an idea, privation is a fact. While looking at the nude body of the girl, the boy tells himself, "She has been castrated"; the girl, while looking at herself determines: "I have been deprived." For the boy, castration is an idea that produces anxiety, the idea that he could lack what is essential; for the girl, privation is a painful realization, the recognition that she lacks something essential that she believed that she had.

> Privation . . . is especially the fact that a woman does not have a penis, that she is deprived of it. This fact, the assumption of this fact, has a constant effect in the evolution of almost all the cases that Freud reports to us. . . . The basis of castration . . . is the apprehension in the real of the absence of the penis in the woman. . . . [Female beings] are castrated in the subjectivity of the subject. In the real, in reality, in what is invoked as real experience, they are deprived.
>
> The very notion of privation . . . implies the symbolization of

the object in the real.... To indicate that something is not there is to suppose its possible presence, that is to say, to introduce in the real ... the sheer symbolic order.

With respect to castration, inasmuch as it is efficacious, experienced, and present in the genesis of a neurosis, it pertains ... to an imaginary object. No castration ... is ever a real castration.[26]

THE SUPER-EGO, THE FRUIT OF OEDIPUS

The super-ego, inheritor of the Oedipus complex, is a figure of the law introjected in the child's unconscious, and dictating, like an interior master, the decisive everyday choices of existence.

The end of the Oedipus complex correlates with the establishment of the law, which, although repressed in the unconscious, is permanent.... The law ... is based in the real, in the kernel that the Oedipus complex leaves behind it ... [a kernel] that we know to be incarnated in each subject in the most diverse, tortured and distorted forms, namely the super ego.[27]

OEDIPUS, A FIGURE OF THE EGO IDEAL

For Lacan, Oedipus is a normative concept, one of the possible figures of the Ego ideal. The Ego ideal is the virile or feminine type that the boy or the girl are destined to assume.

In Oedipus, there is the assumption by the subject of its own sex, that is to say, of what causes a man to assume a virile position and a woman a certain feminine position. Virility and feminization are the two terms that express the essential function of Oedipus. We find ourselves at the point where Oedipus is directly linked to the function of the ego ideal.[28]

It thus does not suffice that after Oedipus the subject arrives at heterosexuality, it is also necessary that the subject, girl or boy, arrives there in such a way as to be situated correctly in relation to the function of the father. This is the crux of the whole problematic of Oedipus.[29]

CASTRATION IS TRANSMITTED FROM THE FATHER TO THE SON

What does it mean to be castrated if not the painful realization that our bodies and our desires are limited? The father that I had, the father that I am, and the son who succeeds me, each must assume the unavoidable castration.

> [C]astration is what strikes the son, is it not also what brings him to accede, by the right path, to what the function of the father is about? . . . And does it not indicate that castration is transmitted from father to son?[30]

DOLTO AND THE PROHIBITION OF INCEST

Dolto asks parents to accept the castration of not regarding their children as an extension of themselves.

> Parents would like to preserve a grasp on their children and plant the fruits of their experience in their mind. This is to transgress the prohibition of incest. The children must abandon everything that has been inculcated from their parents: "*Leave your father and your mother*," which does not mean that the children will not rediscover their heritage in another way, themselves producing what they will have heard, not from their parents but from their experience, from other people in life, on the condition that it is not obligatory, and not in the course of an amorous liaison.[31]

Notes

1. Sigmund Freud, "An Outline of Psycho-analysis," in *The Standard Edition of the Complete Psychological Works of Sigmund Freud Vol. XXIII*, trans. James Strachey (London: The Hogarth Press, 1974), 187, author's emphasis.

2. Sigmund Freud, "From the History of an Infantile Neurosis," in *The Standard Edition of the Complete Psychological Works of Sigmund Freud Vol. XVII*, trans. James Strachey (London: The Hogarth Press, 1974), 86.

3. Sigmund Freud, "From the History of an Infantile Neurosis," in *The Standard Edition of the Complete Psychological Works of Sigmund Freud Vol. XVII*, trans. James Strachey (London: The Hogarth Press, 1974), 119.

4. Sigmund Freud, "Some Character-Types Met With in Psycho-Analytic Work" in *The Standard Edition of the Complete Psychological Works of Sigmund Freud Vol. XIV*, trans. James Strachey (London: The Hogarth Press, 1974), 330.

5. Sigmund Freud, "An Autobiographical Study," in *The Standard Edition of the Complete Psychological Works of Sigmund Freud Vol. XX*, trans. James Strachey (London: The Hogarth Press, 1974), 39.

6. Sigmund Freud, "Two Encyclopaedia Articles," in *The Standard Edition of the Complete Psychological Works of Sigmund Freud Vol. XVIII*, trans. James Strachey (London: The Hogarth Press, 1974), 244.

7. Sigmund Freud, "An Autobiographical Study," in *The Standard Edition of the Complete Psychological Works of Sigmund Freud Vol. XX*, trans. James Strachey (London: The Hogarth Press, 1974), 34.

8. Ibid.

9. Sigmund Freud, "A Child is Being Beaten," in *The Standard Edition of the Complete Psychological Works of Sigmund Freud Vol. XVII*, trans. James Strachey (London: The Hogarth Press, 1974), 188.

10. Ibid., 198.

11. Sigmund Freud, "New Introductory Lectures on Psycho-Analysis," in *The Standard Edition of the Complete Psychological Works of Sigmund Freud Vol. XXII*, trans. James Strachey (London: The Hogarth Press, 1974), 129.

12. Sigmund Freud, "Female Sexuality," in *The Standard Edition of the Complete Psychological Works of Sigmund Freud Vol. XXI*, trans. James Strachey (London: The Hogarth Press, 1974), 228.

13. Sigmund Freud, "The Ego and the Id," in *The Standard Edition of the Complete Psychological Works of Sigmund Freud Vol. XIX*, trans. James Strachey (London: The Hogarth Press, 1974), 34–35.

14. Sigmund Freud, "A Child is Being Beaten," in *The Standard Edition of the Complete Psychological Works of Sigmund Freud Vol. XVII*, trans. James Strachey (London: The Hogarth Press, 1974), 204.

15. Ibid., 193.

16. Sigmund Freud, "New Introductory Lectures on Psycho-Analysis," in *The Standard Edition of the Complete Psychological Works of Sigmund Freud, Vol XXII* (London: The Hogarth Press, 1974), 120.

17. *"Les complexes familiaux dans la formation de l'individu,"* in *Autres Écrits* (Paris: Editions du Seuil, 2001), 47 (unless otherwise noted, all translations from Lacan are ours) .

18. Ibid., 61.

19. *Le Séminaire, Livre IV, La Relation d'objet* (1956–1957) (Paris: Editions du Seuil, 1994), 110.

20. Ibid, 69.

21. *Le Séminaire, Livre V, Les Formations de l'inconscient* (1957–1958) (Paris: Editions du Seuil, 1998), 166.

22. Ibid., 174–75.

23. Le *Séminaire, Livre IV, La Relation d'objet* (1956–1957) (Paris: Editions du Seuil, 1994), 84.

24. Ibid., 81–82.

25. Ibid., 123.

26. Ibid., 218–19.

27. Ibid., 211.

28. *Le Séminaire, Livre V, Les Formations de l'inconscient* (1957–1958) (Paris: Editions du Seuil, 1998), 166.

29. Le Séminaire, Livre IV, La Relation d'objet (1956–1957) (Paris: Editions du Seuil, 1994), 211.

30. *The Seminar of Jacques Lacan: The Other Side of Psychoanalysis* (The Seminar of Jacques Lacan) (Bk. XVII), trans. Russell Grigg (New York: W. W. Norton, 2007), 121 [*Le Séminaire, Livre XVII, L'Envers de la psychanalyse* (1969–1970) (Paris: Editions du Seuil, 1991), 141].

31. Françoise Dolto, *Approches* 40 (1980).

Index